Reengagement

Reengagement

Bringing Students Back to America's Schools

Andrew O. Moore

ROWMAN & LITTLEFIELD
Lanham • Boulder • New York • London

Published by Rowman & Littlefield
A wholly owned subsidiary of The Rowman & Littlefield Publishing Group, Inc.
4501 Forbes Boulevard, Suite 200, Lanham, Maryland 20706
www.rowman.com

Unit A, Whitacre Mews, 26-34 Stannary Street, London SE11 4AB

British Library Cataloguing in Publication Information Available

Library of Congress Cataloging-in-Publication Data

ISBN 978-1-4758-2674-6 (cloth : alk. paper) -- ISBN 978-1-4758-2675-3 (pbk. : alk. paper) -- ISBN 978-1-4758-2676-0 (electronic)

∞ ™ The paper used in this publication meets the minimum requirements of American National Standard for Information Sciences Permanence of Paper for Printed Library Materials, ANSI/NISO Z39.48-1992.

Printed in the United States of America

Contents

Foreword

If there's one value I've seen strong communities share, it's that they offer everyone a chance to reach their potential and make their contribution. A caring community leaves no one behind, and a smart community wastes no one's talents. That's why I am so heartened by the movement growing, in Boston and in America, to bring high school dropouts back to school. It no longer makes sense, ethically or economically, to give up on young people. As the chapters in this book explain, we know how to get them back on track so they can graduate from high school on the way to becoming financially independent workers and productive members of our communities.

Dropout reengagement is the right thing to do for social justice, for public safety, and from an economic perspective as well. Local economies depend on a strong local workforce. With the Baby Boom generation retiring, we can't afford to leave young adults unprepared for twenty-first-century careers. In addition, public budgets are weighed down by the costs associated with the struggles of high school dropouts, from health care to corrections. Reengagement is a smart investment.

If the case for bringing disconnected students back to school is so compelling, why is it only now beginning to get traction? Until recently, high school dropouts were no one's responsibility. School systems did not view those who had left as part of the equation, and the local economy had little use for them. But in Boston and a few other cities, we began to realize the social cost we were paying for leaving these young people adrift. So we began to reach out to high school dropouts to see if they were interested in restarting their education.

As it turned out, many were. And their willingness to return created the enthusiasm necessary for an ambitious reengagement strategy to gather momentum. Outreach helped us to realize that a variety of alternative education programs would be necessary to get these young men and women on the path to community college and beyond. Working with returning students also taught us how to keep other students from dropping out in the first place.

Good data analysis proves critical to these efforts. It starts with measures as simple as counting the number of students who drop out annually. In Boston, we have seen that number fall from over 1,900 annually ten years ago to 700 by the most recent count. Once a reengagement strategy is in full swing, it is important to count the number of students who come in for a first conversation, the number who reenroll, the number who receive appropriate reassignments, and the number who complete their first year back in school.

Equally important: understanding the population that is willing to reengage, by age and by previous academic experience, and with an eye toward overcoming language barriers and accommodating disabilities. Our systems need to be sensitive to the personal circumstances that young adults must manage in order for them to succeed when they return. Thus, community agencies and social service providers become part of the solution.

Despite success so far, we have more to do, in Boston and across the nation. While it represents great progress that we reduced Boston's dropout numbers by more than half, this means that the other half are still on the streets without a ticket to further education or a decent job. Our dropout goal needs to be zero. We need to make steady progress toward that goal every year. And we need a strategy for helping those who are still falling through the cracks.

The publication of this book marks an important new phase for the emerging dropout reengagement movement in America. Sharing knowledge and advancing dialogue about reengagement are critical components of any serious effort to address the dropout crisis and its consequences. Complementing the dialogue, the National League of Cities supports a network of communities that reach out to those who have left school. The national Opportunity Youth movement, led by organizations such as the Aspen Institute and Jobs for the Future, promotes the potential for reengaging out-of-school youth and guiding young adults onto career pathways. Mayors and school superintendents have launched reengagement initiatives that cross traditional boundaries in order to leave no young adult behind.

In Boston, we take pride in helping to lead these urban initiatives and this nationwide movement. We have found that we can, in fact, measure the benefits to our rising generation of young men and women, and to society as a whole. If we hold ourselves accountable collectively, we will make great progress, and we will become stronger as city, state, and national communities.

—Martin J. Walsh, Mayor of Boston

Preface

Seizing the opportunity to gather contributions to a volume on the educational reengagement of out-of-school youth responds to several recognitions about the current landscape of discussion and practice regarding education and youth development. First and foremost, the book provides a means to document local practices and policies in detail, and to convey potential implications for other communities. The past decade has witnessed tremendous innovation in the form of reengagement centers and programs; the stories of that innovation remain largely untold, the lessons from the stories as yet uncaptured.

In a similar vein, spreading effective practices to meet common challenges requires a go-to source of advice based upon experience. To date, only the briefest how-to guidance has appeared in print. As the reengagement field continues to evolve at a rapid pace, a much richer variety of experience has become available. Writing this book offers the opportunity to pull together widely dispersed knowledge and experience into one place.

The passing reference to common challenges above calls out the importance of the subject of education reengagement. Huge investments and high degrees of policy attention now go toward reforming or reinventing high schools for greater efficacy in the twenty-first century, a trend likely to continue. High schools may indeed emerge that no longer fail to meet the needs of the 20 to 50 percent of students who must now find their way on their own through limited alternative and adult education options. But for the foreseeable future, millions of older youth in the United States experience highly tenuous or severed relationships with credentialing pathways, and they often need assistance to reengage.

The emerging reengagement field still finds itself in an early stage of development, with considerable experimentation underway. Given the variety of local conditions and relatively limited number of formalized strategies, no clear trajectory presents itself as the best means to fill a previously unfulfilled niche for systematic reengagement of out-of-school youth. The generally preferred frame of a citywide solution competes with well-established and often different jurisdictional boundaries involving school districts, community college catchment areas, and workforce development regions—not to mention the frequently underdeveloped relationship between city government leaders and local school officials.

By absorbing this book in whole or in part, the reader will come away with a far better sense of the breadth, depth, lessons to date, and continuing challenges in the emerging field of education reengagement. Chapters variously provide useful principles, details on practices, and frames of analysis to consider.

Most readers should emerge from reading, convinced of the importance of spreading and scaling systematic reengagement strategies in communities of all sizes. Some may grow convinced of the highly leverageable potential of relatively low-cost reengagement interventions. And many will emerge with new and evolved practice and policy questions, the process of responding to which will contribute to further enrichment and improvement of the field.

Introduction

Welcome to the first volume-length treatment of the emerging topic of educational reengagement of out-of-school youth. This is a book by practitioners, written for other practitioners and for policymakers and researchers. It captures much of the best experience, passion, and as yet unresolved issues concerning the present *art and science* of reengagement.

Art—because reengagement depends crucially upon the central, very human relationships that professional youth workers create with out-of-school youth.

Science—because reengagement has only grown and spread thanks to supporting policies and close analysis of data.

The reengagement approach has emerged to meet the supports and services needs of young people ages sixteen to twenty-four who have left school prior to high school graduation—for reasons ranging from boredom to "push-out" due to school discipline regimes. Absent a concerted reengagement effort, such young people must rely mostly on their own and peer group resources and referrals to find their way back to school.

In contrast, comprehensive reengagement approaches embrace five main functions: outreach to the known pool of dropouts, often complemented by an open-door policy for self-motivated youth; assessment of educational standing and psychosocial needs; referral to a "best fit" education option as well as wraparound support services; support to reenroll in that best-fit option; and support to stay enrolled for at least the subsequent year. Variety appears in the way that cities, school districts, and their partners manage these functions.

The development of coordinated citywide efforts to reengage out-of-school youth on positive educational pathways—in several dozen cities in recent years—spurred the effort to document practice and policy considerations. As a public policy innovation, reengagement programs involve school districts, city governments, community colleges, and others in filling a previously unfilled niche of local infrastructure. Within that new niche, reengagement programs bring the proven principles of positive youth development to a population otherwise consigned to long-term struggles to survive in the economy as well as in community and family life.

This book describes the hard-won early triumphs of reengagement in several cities, provides practical advice from a variety of perspectives for those seeking to launch or formalize local reengagement efforts, and describes how reengagement at scale could help solve the crisis of unfulfilled potential represented in America's millions of young people without high school credentials. Importantly, the book features the voices and stories of front-line practitioners and young people.

SCOPE AND STRUCTURE

This volume provides a new means through which to unleash the energy that suffuses the NLC Reengagement Network, a power previously visible at national and regional meetings and through a remarkably high degree of collegial peer support. Twenty-eight people associated with the Network responded to the call to distill contributions from recent lived experience. Their writing appears in eighteen separate chapters.

The book's first section, Dimensions of Reengagement, sets reengagement issues in context and provides illustrative examples of reengagement center start-up, as well as operating approaches and accomplishments. The start-up stories come from the varied settings of Allentown, Pennsylvania, and Washington, DC. Key organizers and analysts of reengagement in Boston explain the combination of community organizing and programming that has significantly reduced dropout rates in that city. By special arrangement with Next America, the section closes with Waiting for Daniel, a moving profile of one young man's reengagement.

The second section, Important Techniques in Reengagement, provides highly practical advice for those seeking to launch, expand, or improve local efforts. The section begins with complementary reports from Denver, Dubuque, and New York City on direct outreach to out-of-school youth, an essential element of any reengagement project. From a structural level, Los Angeles and Nashville provide examples of what it takes for institutional partners to come together to support reengagement.

Also in this section, an indigenous voice offers principles for successful reengagement of two overrepresented groups within the out-of-school youth population, American Indians and Latinos. And one of the most experienced reengagement specialists in the nation conveys lessons for program staff, from the front lines.

The third major section, Emerging, Promising Practices in Reengagement, delves into several of the innovative practices and connections programs have pursued more recently to enhance outcomes. From Portland, Oregon, comes a description of efforts to integrate workforce development and education, and from Reno, Nevada, the story of embracing student voice; from Los Angeles, embracing online and blended learning. From multiple perspectives, authors discuss early findings about the potential for reengaging more out-of-school youth directly into postsecondary education or postsecondary-oriented pathways.

The concluding chapter, Future Prospects, lays out major next steps, challenges, and opportunities for the reengagement field. Observations about the future stem from the realization that, with the exception of local developments in Washington State supported by state government, reengagement has grown and spread opportunistically to date. As in other breakout areas of new policy, questions now arise about how best to build upon the impressive start provided by a group of founders and start-up specialists toward sustained growth and impact.

One important qualification: though broad, the scope of this book does not address some key portions of the broader "reengagement ecosystem." Thus, with the exception of the attention to Gateway to College in chapter 14, no chapter here treats one common experience across the nation, in which alternative schools themselves recruit and retain students without benefit of an entity filling the reengagement niche. Nor does the book explore the actual operations of the alternative schools and adult education programs that receive referrals from reengagement centers and programs.

ANTECEDENTS AND SUPPORTS

The subject matter in this book harkens back at least as far as incisive analyses such as Michelle Fine's *Framing Dropouts*, and draws as well upon recent and ongoing studies by practically oriented members of the academy such as Andrew Sum, Paul Harrington, Russell Rumberger, Jon Zaff, and Robert Balfanz and colleagues. The Millenium Group International broke important ground via its development of the U.S. Department of Education Resource Guide on reengagement centers.

National groups such as the American Youth Policy Forum, Jobs for the Future, and the National Youth Employment Coalition helped set the stage and context for the spread of reengagement. Each has helped generate a substantial body of literature and program profiles on reengagement and alternative education. Networks of programs supported through national technical assistance initiatives of such organizations, and by the National League of Cities, have provided essential grounds for experimentation and program development.

As a practical matter, early support from the Charles Stewart Mott Foundation and more recent, ongoing support from the Annie E. Casey Foundation made time available to conceive, develop, and edit this book. Earlier, support from the Bill & Melinda Gates Foundation for the Alternative High School Initiative planted reengagement seeds. The Youth Transition Funders Group—Multiple Pathways to Graduation Work Group, in which these foundations participate, has consistently signaled interest and support.

The action tank orientation of the National League of Cities Institute for Youth, Education, and Families flexed helpfully to permit creation of the book. Institute director Clifford Johnson provided key insight and guidance at all stages. Talented interns Samuel Weinstock, Marleyna Greene, and Lauren Greenawalt each helped shape the annual census that NLC uses to understand the growth and dynamics of reengagement. Graduate fellow Zachia Nazarzai played essential roles in the run-up to finalizing the manuscript, including updating reengagement census figures, fact checking, checking citations, and preparing the resources and references section.

The authors who went above and beyond their day-to-day roles to prepare outlines and chapters, and to respond to sometimes extensive proposed edits, also deserve a deep bow of respect and thanks. Except for one journalist and a small number of researchers, almost no one on the extensive list of contributors "gets paid to write" as a function of his or her normal job. That each of the authors rose above daily challenges and pressures to tell their story speaks volumes about them as professionals, and indeed as the vanguard of the reengagement movement.

I

Dimensions of Engagement

Chapter One

Reengagement as an Issue, and an Emerging Field of Practice and Policy

Andrew O. Moore

Before evoking the creative ferment and variety of practice and policy in the still-new field of education reengagement, it helps to review a brief history of the field, as well as driving issues and rationales. Overall, reengagement has experienced rapid growth to date, which a stepwise model or metaphor may capture best. As in other social and educational policy arenas, following an initial step of assembling a new suite of services, additional steps followed. In this case, steps included early adoption in several more cities, innovation in modes of delivery, and at least one quantum leap from local to state policy.

Temporarily isolating out reengagement as an issue—from the swirl of related concerns such as graduation rate accountability, high-stakes testing, absenteeism, school discipline policies, youths' need for work experience, and more—has led to some variety in local responses within a framework of similar conceptual hypotheses, about what it takes to return out-of-school youth to educational pathways. Across the country, embracing a systematic approach to reengagement has involved carving out a new niche or operating space, the specific need for which few previously recognized.

SCALING AND SCOPING THE ISSUE

The U.S. Department of Education's 2014 resource guide for reengagement centers, *Bringing Students Back to the Center*—the publication of which signaled the arrival of reengagement as an issue for federal policy consideration—thoroughly conveys the scale and several key dimensions of the reengagement issue, as follows:

Nationally, 1.8 million young adults aged 16–21 are not enrolled in school or have not finished their high school education. Nearly 400,000 students drop out of high school each year. Despite recent gains, graduation rates are 79% or lower in over half the states, and significant attainment gaps persist for urban, minority, immigrant, and low-income youth. African-American and Hispanic students appear somewhat more successful than in the past, but large disparities in comparison to White and Asian students still exist. Urban areas demonstrate less success than suburban locations. Persistently, data confirm graduation gaps identifiable by race, ethnicity, immigrant status, family income, disabilities, and English proficiency. [1]

The population of potentially reengaged students exists outside the walls of school buildings, and sometimes even outside of student information databases. In most places, the students who districts might reengage live in a zone of invisibility, for a variety of reasons hard to pin down and perhaps best framed for the moment in a series of questions.

Have resource constraints and accountability structures forced attention solely to those students still attending school, and prevented allocating staff time to reenroll those who have stopped attending? Have the constituents of school districts, and overlapping populations of city government constituents, come to define the scope of local education in a way that does not include *all* children and youth? How has the delegation of policy and political responsibility for education to local education agencies, and the typically lesser involvement of other levels of government, contributed to the overriding focus on in-school youth?

Beyond these questions, nationwide, the most common policy response to the sheer numbers of out-of-school older youth involves what one could characterize fairly as indirect efforts to stem the flow of young people leaving school. Doubtless, much room exists to improve student engagement significantly to prevent disengaging and dropping out, through means such as changes in classroom practices and school structure, instituting school-based supports, and regularizing practices such as dual enrollment in postsecondary courses.

However, more years will pass before such changes result in anything approximating "leak-proof" high schools, and the young people who do "leak out" in the meantime need a different policy and practice response if universal education constitutes the goal. In addition, hundreds of thousands of out-of-school young people already stand in need of reengagement supports and services. In the normal course of events, only a fraction of these will attain a high school diploma or the equivalent, leaving many others to fare poorly in a labor market that increasingly demands a postsecondary credential as a condition of entry.

A BRIEF HISTORY OF THE REENGAGEMENT FIELD

Systematic local responses to the need to reengage out-of-school youth emerged in their present form over the past decade. The first tier of activity, in the 2005-07 time period, involved the development of one-stop, physical reengagement centers in cities of varying sizes. Notably, this first tier included Dayton, Ohio's Fast Forward Center; the Philadelphia Reengagement Center; and the Boston Reengagement Center, the latter as a step beyond the city's original Project ReConnect.

The latter two efforts stemmed in considerable part from comprehensive local analyses and strategy development to address the dropout crisis, Dayton's from a similarly comprehensive effort supported by a special revenue source from surrounding Montgomery County. Other early activity took shape in Newark, New Jersey, in the form of the Youth Education and Employment Success (YE2S) Center, subsequently replicated in Camden and Trenton by Rutgers University Cooperative Extension.

In the first three centers, sponsorship and sources of staffing varied considerably, setting a pattern for future developments. Sinclair Community College hosts Fast Forward, and refers students mostly to alternative schools outside local school districts. The School District of Philadelphia hosts the local center in the district's headquarters building and has obtained additional staffing in-kind from among child welfare experts at the city's Department of Human Services. The Boston Public Schools and Boston Private Industry Council collaborated to plan, operate, and staff a center with public resources and philanthropic donations.

In a development nearly parallel in time, the statewide nonprofit organization Colorado Youth for a Change pioneered the use of specialized reengagement staff deployed throughout the community. First with Denver Public Schools and subsequently with other districts as well, Colorado Youth for a Change also innovated by structuring annual performance-based contracts with districts.

In other words, under the contract, the districts pay the organization a specific amount for each student who reenrolled successfully. At the outset, for instance, the typical contracted per-student payment was in the range of $1,000, as against the approximately $7,000 in per-pupil funding the district would then draw down from the state.

With a few operating models in existence and ongoing discussion underway in multiple other jurisdictions about potential strategies to reengage disconnected youth, in 2011 the National League of Cities Institute for Youth, Education, and Families—utilizing support from the Charles Stewart Mott Foundation for staff time—put out a call for interest in forming a mutually supportive, virtual peer network.

Interest proved strong, and within a few months of making initial connections via conference call and webinar, Boston offered to host the first national reengagement convening. Some thirty-five participants from operating centers and programs, as well as prospective sites such as Omaha, Nebraska, Dubuque, Iowa, and Washington, D.C., attended.

The formation of the Reengagement Network and the first national gathering helped bring to light and spur additional tiers of recognized practice. These included New York City's Referral Centers for High School Alternatives—one per borough—and Portland's centralized Reconnection Center. In the widely varying circumstances of the two cities, the school district operates the centers. Thereafter, Chicago Public Schools' 2013 creation of three (now four) Student Outreach and Reengagement (SOAR) centers drew considerable inspiration from these district-led approaches.

With continued refraction of reengagement approaches through local context, still other models have emerged. Omaha, Nebraska, created the first foundation-funded reengagement center in 2011, dubbed Direction Diploma or D2. Dubuque, Iowa, borrowed from the Colorado experience to institute ReEngage Dubuque as a deployed staff model in 2012, with support from a partnership involving the city government, community foundation, school district, and community college. Colorado Youth for a Change innovated further with web-based and public service announcement–based "Drop In" Campaigns that sought to enlist the power of technology and young people's affinity for texting, Facebook, and Twitter.

Meanwhile, the state legislature in Washington had passed House Bill 1418 in 2010. This commissioned a small staff at the Office of the State Superintendent of Public Instruction to launch the first "Open Doors" reengagement programs through model contracts and interlocal agreements. This development constituted the first major reengagement beachhead in state policy, and indeed has led to the establishment or formalization of several dozen Open Doors efforts in Washington cities, school districts, and community colleges.

Across these tiers of development, the Reengagement Network has served as a critical hub for exchanging policy and practice information, procedures, and advice. The Network has achieved and sustained this role through an ongoing series of large group conference phone calls and task force meetings, and has facilitated cross-center visits and national convenings. Helpful support from the Annie E. Casey Foundation supplemented the effort, and lead reengagement organizations in Denver, Los Angeles, and Portland stepped forward to host the larger meetings.

Two additional factors informed and contributed to the growth of reengagement practices. The U.S. Department of Education's five-year High School Graduation Initiative (HSGI) grants came to some two dozen school districts in 2010, with a requirement to scale up dropout prevention *and* recovery activity. The Washoe County School District in Reno, Nevada, provides one prominent example of reengagement centers first established under an HSGI grant.

Also, the establishment of the Opportunity Youth Incentive Fund (OYIF) followed closely on the move to the Aspen Institute of a White House–initiated project on reengaging Opportunity Youth. OYIF regranted planning and scale-up funds to an initial twenty-one sites. Half of these already included reengagement centers or programs as one aspect of their efforts to place Opportunity Youth on sound career pathways. The grants provided reinforcement and held the promise of growth of added local alternative education pathways. And additional OYIF sites such as Tucson, Arizona, determined to add reengagement capacity as the initial step on a career pathway continuum.

THE BROADER REENGAGEMENT ECOSYSTEM

Throughout the existing Network and in potential sites for further development, almost any conversation about the basic reengagement functions of outreach, assessment, and referral spills over quickly into what one might call the broader reengagement ecosystem.

Reengagement centers and programs do not operate in isolation. Indeed, they depend heavily upon other agencies to provide a range of wraparound services and upon schools to reenroll students. Taking a system or ecosystem view brings into focus system elements such as the local range of education options, sources of assistance for psychosocial needs, sources of work and job training, and linkages to postsecondary credentialing pathways.

Of perhaps highest importance, reengagement programs cannot complete the handoff of out-of-school youth back into school without access to some range of education options in which those students could complete a high-school-level credential or otherwise accelerate forward through dual enrollment in college. Operationally, every reengagement program worth its salt must obtain an intimate knowledge of the emphasis and capacity of available local options in order to recommend the placement most likely to work out for each student.

However, again at the policy or system level, a structural shortage of education options bedevils almost every local reengagement effort. Seventy-five percent of school districts in the United States operate only one high school. Even in larger districts, one or a very small number of in-district alternative options exist. Community-based school options run by nonprofit organizations in the youth development sector, as well as charter schools that specialize in enrolling formerly out-of-school youth, typically have very limited capacity to receive additional referrals. And only the rare city or district pursues an explicit strategy to expand such options.

This consistent shortfall of education options to meet the reengagement need constitutes another facet of the overriding policy emphasis on dropout prevention and reform of existing high schools. This has led some districts and reengagement programs to create schools-within-schools or special programs of support to ease the otherwise unlikely return of out-of-school youth to the building they left. More broadly, reengagement advocates seek to push local policy development toward expanding options by offering palpable human demonstrations and statistics regarding the need.

As the idea gathers steam, Reengagement Network results and participation to date provide encouragement. The annual reengagement census documents growth across a changing set of several dozen centers and programs; see table 1.1 for a three-year comparison. By the 2014-15 school year, aggregate responses showed seventeen programs making initial contact with nearly twenty-four thousand young people.

Of these, reengagement programs placed more than thirteen thousand students back into school, and 75 percent of those placed completed their studies or persisted for the full school year. For another point of reference, more than 250 people from thirty-eight cities in twenty-two states attended the 2014 Reengagement Plus convening, doubling the size from the previous year.

Table 1.1.

	2013	2014	2015
Sites reporting	13 of 13	15 of 17	17 of 18
Initial contact with center or program	22,409	23,475	23,617
Reenrolled in school	9,528	11,592	13,278
Persisted through end of year or completed	71%	70%	75%

This chapter's review of circumstances and developments illustrates the creative ferment informing the reengagement field, even as it sketches some of the field's ongoing challenges. The highly localized pattern of program development has ensured strong fits with local context, and has, for instance, enlisted support from across the community leadership ranks of mayors, school superintendents, businesspeople, nonprofit executives, and workforce agency and community foundation heads.

At present, the diversity of the field constitutes one of its major strengths. Drawing upon a different ecological metaphor than that cited above, the diversity of local approaches provides a rich seedbed from which to spread ideas further across the national landscape. As those ideas spread, the field must embrace the opportunity to codify the best or most promising practices to support replication and growth with fidelity to an effective model.

NOTE

1. Leslie Rennie-Hill et al., *Bringing Students Back to the Center*, U.S. Department of Education (November 2014), in turn drawing upon National Governors Association 2007 and America's Promise Alliance, *Building a Grad Nation: Progress and Challenge in Ending the High School Dropout Epidemic* (2012).

Chapter Two

Illustrative Profiles of Reengagement Approaches

Andrew O. Moore

Reengaging students who have left school, through staffed drop-in centers or outreach efforts, represents a dynamic new development for the education and youth development fields in the United States. The reengagement centers and programs springing up across the nation in recent years fill a previously little-noticed niche for the large pool of former students still of an age to receive per-pupil support from state governments, and who local districts could presumably accommodate.

A healthy variety constitutes one of the notable characteristics of the budding reengagement movement—in approach, and in creative adaptation to local context. Certain functional elements remain the same, including outreach to the known pool of dropouts; assessment of educational and psychosocial needs; referrals to meet those needs; support to reenroll in a "best fit" option; and support to stay enrolled for at least one year. Taking those commonalities as understood, this chapter offers a virtual tour across several reengagement sites to highlight the variety and creativity visible across the country.

CHICAGO'S SOAR CENTERS: EMBODYING THE ONE-STOP APPROACH

With the launch of what has grown into a network of four dropout reengagement centers beginning in January 2013, Chicago joined the ranks of cities that use highly accessible physical locations to connect out-of-school youth and their families with services that enable the youth to obtain a diploma or

GED. Such "one-stop" approaches constitute one of the most common across the Reengagement Network.

Key aspects of the organization of Chicago's centers draw upon experience from cities around the nation, and connect strongly with local context and related initiatives. Chicago Public Schools (CPS), which operates as a city agency, conceived and developed what it calls the Student Outreach and Reengagement (SOAR) centers, and contracts with a community-based organization to operate each of the four centers.

The City of Chicago built the SOAR centers as one aspect of Mayor Rahm Emanuel's citywide violence reduction strategy. The SOAR effort also connects to state-level policy, receiving partial funding support from a grant provided by the State of Illinois under the Truants' Alternative and Optional Education Program (TAOEP).[1]

At another level, Chicago's foray into reengagement confirmed the benefits of linking to current district leadership initiatives to expand alternative school options, as well as outreach to dropouts. Both new directions enjoyed the strong support of CPS's then-recently appointed CEO and the school board.

The SOAR centers use several means to locate dropouts. Reengagement specialists—four at each center—receive a list of students who have withdrawn from Chicago public schools or show signs of chronic truancy. The specialists also work with counselors at nearby schools to identify dropouts or truants, and they receive ongoing referrals as well.

All returning students undergo an intake assessment created by the center's director to identify barriers to school success; results of the assessment frequently prompt referrals to supportive services. A reengagement facilitator reviews the student's transcript to determine graduation needs and develops a graduation plan. Prior to school placement, students must complete a rigorous nine-day "character development" workshop, which includes a service-learning project.

If a school placement is not available immediately, the SOAR centers provide online credit recovery options for "old and close" students—that is, those who have almost enough credits to graduate with a diploma. "Old and far" students, through a partnership with the Community College of Chicago, have access to GED instruction.

Reengagement specialists meet with each student weekly to ensure that the students stay on track toward their goals. Counselors also meet with each student weekly in a group or individual session. Staff report the most success to date with "old and far" students who have been out of school for at least one year, because these young people come to the centers highly motivated to obtain a diploma.

Overall, the first three Chicago SOAR centers made initial contact with more than six hundred students during their first six months of operation. Of these, one-third (219) completed the character development workshop—and of that group, 154, or 24 percent of the students originally contacted, made a successful transition into a school, online learning, or GED program.

Another fifty-three former dropouts enrolled in a workforce development program that also provided after-school jobs and mentoring. Since then, the number of youth engaging with the center annually has grown considerably. In the 2014-15 academic year, the SOAR centers connected with 2,839 out-of-school youth and placed 2,194 of them in an educational program.

Chicago's earliest experience propelled CPS staff to work with several local organizations to expand the services available to youth. In fall 2013, the SOAR centers contracted with the Teen Outreach Program to provide workshops, service-learning opportunities, and stipends. In addition, district staff worked with their colleagues at the centers to change the nature of initial intake workshops, to make them "less like school" and thus more welcoming.

Current partners facilitating workshops include Central State SER and Phalanx Family Services. Both organizations have strong histories of providing workforce training and social-emotional learning supports to youth and adults in the Chicago area.

DENVER: MAYORAL LEADERSHIP AND OBTAINING SERVICES THROUGH PARTNERSHIP

Denver's approach to reengagement features significant involvement across sectors—the public schools, city government, and nonprofit organizations in particular. Bespeaking the city's involvement, Mayor Michael B. Hancock welcomed the Reengagement Network to Denver in 2012 with a compelling, threefold explanation of why he prioritizes confronting the dropout problem as essential to overcoming economic challenges facing his city.

Developing effective reengagement strategies, emphasized the mayor, is first and foremost the right thing to do. He added that it is too costly to ignore the problem. And he concluded that investing in children and youth to close the achievement gap also provides a key means to narrow the gap between the skills of adult workers and the jobs that the city needs to fill.

"By developing reengagement strategies, we remind young people that they matter, that they're important to the fabric of our city," Mayor Hancock declared. When meeting with business and community groups, Mayor Hancock often asks the audience to name a single economic problem facing the city that isn't in some way connected to the goal of making sure everyone graduates from high school. The response, he says, is almost invariably silence.

From mayoral, school district, and nonprofit leadership, a considerable reengagement tide has arisen. In Denver and other Colorado cities, dropout reengagement operates as more of an intensive outreach and support process rather than a physical center or location. For instance, Denver Public Schools, working through a partnership contract with the nonprofit Colorado Youth for a Change, reaches out to dropouts within the first twenty-four hours of formal exit from high school.

An expanded number of schools offering more intensive student supports, along with engagement or multiple pathway centers for some students, provide more options within Denver Public Schools for recent dropouts to find a school environment that meets their needs. In the 2014-15 academic year, Colorado Youth for a Change helped 493 students reenroll in a program to continue their education.

In the Denver suburbs, Jefferson County Public Schools has set up an internal district office to focus on reengagement, and crafted new procedures regarding student exits from high school. Boulder's school district employs reengagement and alternative schools in its drive to reduce the number of dropouts annually to zero. And as one reengaged student at the Aurora, Colorado, Futures Academy noted during a site visit by Reengagement Network members, "At my high school, no one was paying attention to my absences until I got a call from [the school]."

RENO AND DUBUQUE: REENGAGEMENT IN SMALLER CITIES

"Two staff members of the Reengagement Center provided my only support. Otherwise I was alone. Because of them, I'm graduating in June 2015 with my class." These sad yet inspiring words came from Tara Ebbs, a beneficiary of one of the Washoe County, Nevada Reengagement Centers in Reno, who had reenrolled at Washoe Innovations High School in the 2012-13 school year. Reno, the major city in Washoe County, constitutes one of the smaller jurisdictions to institute one-stop-style reengagement practices. Another small city, Dubuque, Iowa, has opted to deploy reengagement coaches at large.

Reno: A Case Management Style Approach

For context, the 2013 graduating cohort in Washoe County saw 608 students leave at some time during high school, and the district recorded more than 700 students leaving during the 2013-14 academic year. With these numbers in mind, Washoe County embarked on efforts to offer retooled and better alternative high school settings, including a Big Picture Learning model school and schools-within-schools at each of the local campuses.

In their first three full years of operation, with four to six operating sites and a staff of up to seven, the Washoe Reengagement Centers have reconnected about one-third of the pool of students who left school recently in the sprawling county. And a notable 74 percent of the students reenrolled through the Centers have "stuck it out" in school for at least the balance of the school year, placing Washoe County on par with the national "stick rate" for reengagement centers. Largely returning to alternative settings, about 20 percent of Washoe's reenrolled students immediately earned credits at a rate similar to that of traditional high school students.

Each year in Reno, reengagement staff connect with more than 160 out-of-school youth. This average obscures a steady increase in the number of youth who connect with one of the reengagement centers; meanwhile, the percentage of youth contacted who reconnect with an educational program has fluctuated. And for students who "enroll" at one of the reengagement centers and do not connect to an educational option, the district cannot receive per-pupil student funding. For instance, in the 2014 to 2015 school year, 41 percent of students contacted enrolled solely in a reengagement center as a first step.

To meet the demand, Washoe County's initial staffing consisted of three reengagement specialists and three family advocates. The reengagement specialists held responsibility for outreach to former students whom the district identified as having left school. Family advocates provided case management services to reenrolling students and their families. The roles and responsibilities of reengagement staff at the center have evolved, and all family advocate positions have now converted to reengagement specialist positions.

Reengagement specialists now conduct outreach to students who have dropped out, as well as those who are at risk of dropping out as indicated by the district's early warning system. The specialists also receive referrals from each school's problem-solving team—most often the Multi-Tiered Systems of Support team or the Intervention Assistance Team. Once specialists contact students successfully, the focus shifts to case management. As part of the latter support process, students and their families frequently receive referrals to community partners to address immediate physical and mental health needs.

Dubuque: We Want All Our Young People to Succeed

Halfway across the country, leaders in Dubuque, Iowa—a city of sixty thousand with a high school graduation rate of 88 percent—asked, Does it matter if three hundred to five hundred sixteen-to-twenty-one-year-olds have not received a high school diploma? The answer: Yes, it does matter, we want all our young people to succeed.

That definitive answer led to the creation of Re-Engage Dubuque, supported by a partnership between the City of Dubuque, Dubuque Community Schools, the Community Foundation of Greater Dubuque, and Northeast Iowa Community College (NICC). Re-Engage Dubuque's approach incorporates a combination of virtual options, such as allowing students to earn credits through online courses, with a wide-ranging outreach effort.

In mid-February 2014, the Dubuque partners paused briefly to assemble, report, and celebrate results of the first eighteen months of operation. Since August 2012, the initiative's coaches had connected with 190 dropouts and enrolled 180 of them in online courses, alternative and traditional high schools, or adult education programs. Of those reenrolled, 37 percent had received a high school diploma or a high school equivalency diploma.

Dubuque mayor Roy Buol led the celebration of success to date, noting that "while dropout prevention is a priority, it is equally important to help youth and adults connect back into education opportunities . . . Re-Engage Dubuque contributes greatly to the sustainability goals of our community. To be a viable, equitable community, it is critically important to reengage our disconnected young citizens." School superintendent Stan Rheingans, whose district strategic plan includes a reengagement plank, added that the school district wants to ensure the success of the "other 11 percent" [who do not graduate on time]. This partnership exists to show those students that there is a path to success for them."

Eric Dregne, vice president of the Community Foundation, calculated that the initial investment of $200,000 from the partners would produce significant positive economic impacts over time. These include $917,000 in additional taxes paid, and a projected $462,000 in additional earnings.

Lead Re-Engage Dubuque organizers from the schools, foundation, and community college pointed to three key developments to explain this strong early success record:

- *Building strong local alliances*: The city and the foundation folded Re-Engage Dubuque into the existing Project HOPE Initiative—supported by $70,000 per year in city funding—and recruited other partners. The schools oversee staff and operational needs; the college provides high school equivalency instruction; and the foundation provides small-scale funding to cover incidental costs that reenrolled students incur.
- *Identifying participation barriers and creating solutions*: The team of two talented reengagement coaches connects students with academic and social supports, and even provides transportation if needed. A NICC staff member commented, "Coaches are the hub of our wheel. [We emphasize] the handoff from reengagement coaches to NICC career coaches."

- *Looking for students where they are*: Coaches spend most of their time circulating throughout the community pursuing students from the district's dropout list.

WASHINGTON STATE: OPEN DOORS YOUTH REENGAGEMENT

Through a May 20, 2013, statewide meeting among representatives of eighty-eight school districts, community colleges, community-based organization partners, and the City of Seattle, Washington State surged into new prominence in the national dropout reengagement field.

Indeed, Washington stands in a place of its own since the passage of Washington House Bill 1418[2] and the establishment of the Open Doors Youth Reengagement[3] system in state policy. This policy enables state start-up funding to flow to Open Doors sites, and to knit the sites together in a peer-learning network. Open Doors confirms the potential contribution of state policy and funding to the rapid scaling of reengagement efforts. In the 2013-14 school year alone, more than four thousand students reenrolled at Open Doors sites.

Notably, and somewhat distinct from dropout reengagement approaches in other states, Washington State's Open Doors programs combine the dropout outreach and assessment functions with alternative education at one site. Open Doors programs must offer academic instruction, case management, counseling, resource and referral services, and the opportunity to enroll in college courses tuition-free if the program provider is a college.

The founding program coordinator once noted that financial motivation can match the drive for youth development: a state cost study found $250 million in savings to public coffers for every group of six hundred reengaged former dropouts. With more than thirty thousand students coded as dropped out over the 2010-13 time period statewide, the total savings from effective, scaled-up reengagement could become huge.

Whereas the Open Doors network has grown to include forty distinct programs, a closer look at the three initial Open Doors Reengagement programs provides insight into the variety of local approaches. Perhaps most notably, each of these three differs in terms of the lead sponsor role. This variety is consistent with the breadth of opportunity provided by Open Doors's policy framework, which allows school districts to enter into interlocal agreements with a qualifying organization.

- GRAVITY High School operated by Education Service District 113 took shape as a consortium model involving twenty-five school districts and more than 220 students in a large region southwest of Seattle.

- The Kent School District launched iGRAD in partnership with Green River Community College, in the South Puget Sound area. iGRAD offers three high school diploma options—students can earn a diploma from the Kent district, the state, or a GED—at its convenient location in a shopping mall. Green River CC professors teach GED courses four days per week. iGRAD offers classes in three different segments during the day—morning, afternoon, and evening—and also offers classes online. iGRAD provides these classes and options for more than five hundred students.
- The Gateway to College[4] program at Lake Washington Institute of Technology constitutes the only one of the first three Open Doors that a community college operates directly. The Institute has developed interlocal agreements with twenty-three school districts to operate what Washington State calls an accredited special purpose high school. Some two hundred on-track students may enroll in the Institute directly. Another two hundred start in Gateway to College.

Regardless, Gateway students at Lake Washington experience hands-on technical training and dual-credit-earning opportunities. Gateway students also receive more intensive case management than most. Students may earn one of three types of diplomas—a regular high school diploma, an adult high school diploma, or a diploma simultaneous with an associate's degree (via Washington HB 1758). In its first year, the Institute saw 60 percent of students persist from one fall term to the next, and that rate has increased with time.

Taken together, the first three programs' commonalities in operations exemplify a comment that state superintendent Randy Dorn made at the May 2013 meeting. Noting that the statewide extended graduation rate (four-, five-, and six-year graduations) is 80 percent, "the next 5% [of graduates] will cost more, and will require a relationship" with caring adults consistent with best practices in the youth development field.

The preceding brief program profiles provide an initial sense of the rich variety of approaches in use across the dropout reengagement field—and these sites collectively represent a small yet significant portion of the known reengagement activity across the nation. The one-stop centers of Chicago and Reno, the deployed youth coaches of Denver and Dubuque, and the school- and college-linked offerings in Washington State all proceed with similar aims and show promising early results. Keeping these dynamic local efforts in mind helps inform the sense of the potential for growing the reengagement field.

NOTES

1. "Illinois State Board of Education, Special Education Services—TAOEP," accessed September 21, 2015, http://www.isbe.net/spec-ed/html/taoep.htm.

2. "Washington State Legislature: Statewide Dropout Reengagement Program," accessed September 21, 2015, http://apps.leg.wa.gov/rcw/default.aspx?cite=28A.175.100.

3. "State of Washington, Office of Superintendent of Public Instruction: Open Doors Youth Reengagement," accessed September 21, 2015, http://www.k12.wa.us/GATE/SupportingStudents/StudentRetrieval.aspx.

4. "Lake Washington Institute of Technology, Gateway to College," http://www.lwtech.edu/explore_our_programs/high_school_programs/gateway_to_college.aspx.

Chapter Three

What Did It Take to Start Up in Washington, DC?

Celine Fejeran

Washington, DC, has long stood on the forefront of national education reform efforts, pioneering universal access to pre-K education, as well as a bold human capital initiative to drive improvements in K–12 education. And in October 2014, then-mayor Vincent C. Gray declared, "We can't stop there—not if we're serious about helping all young people succeed, from cradle to career."

Addressing a standing-room-only crowd at the ReEngagement Center (REC) ribbon cutting, Gray continued, "We cannot afford financially and morally to lose our young people, and they cannot afford to have us give up on them. Our dropout numbers are sobering—but they are also numbers we can do something about."

Consistent with the mayor's call to action, this chapter recounts the collective effort by which Washington, D.C., launched its first REC, exploring: 1) the elements in place that created the opportunity to launch; 2) core design features and targeted partnerships critical for startup; and 3) postlaunch reflections as efforts shift from startup to sustainability. Systematic planning has produced notable early results. In its first year of operation, the DC REC connected with approximately six hundred dropouts ages sixteen to twenty-four, successfully reenrolled just shy of two hundred, and achieved a "stick rate" of 74 percent.

A WINDOW OF OPPORTUNITY: THE CONVERGENCE OF
CHAMPIONS, DATA, AND A BLUEPRINT

According to John W. Kingdon's Policy Window theory,[1] three "streams" must align to address any public issue: 1) political—Are officials willing and able to make a change? 2) problem—Is the condition defined and considered a problem? 3) policy—Is there a feasible solution? The convergence of these three streams in DC created a window of opportunity for the REC to become a reality.

For years, advocates for disconnected youth in Washington, D.C., championed the issue of reconnection by convening and educating stakeholders on the need to focus on this critical population. These advocacy efforts created a steady drumbeat of support and laid the groundwork for the issue to take root in the Office of the Deputy Mayor for Education (DME) as a top-level priority in 2011.

Simultaneously, an emerging coalition of cross-sector leaders (later to take shape as the district's collective impact partnership, Raise DC) elevated reconnection as one of the city's five overarching educational goals. These leaders also established the Disconnected Youth Change Network (DYCN) as the first sustained gathering of government, direct-service nonprofit, education, advocacy, and philanthropic leaders all focused specifically on this issue.

In tandem with the emerging coalition of champions, a growing body of local research began to dig deeper into the dynamics of D.C.'s disengaged population. In 2011, the Brookings Institution released its groundbreaking brief, *Strengthening Educational and Career Pathways for D.C. Youth*,[2] which found that nearly one in ten sixteen-to-twenty-four-year-olds in D.C. were not in school and not working. This research reignited public discourse around this challenge.

Building on the Brookings research, the D.C. Office of the State Superintendent of Education (OSSE) utilized its Statewide Longitudinal Education Data system to take a deeper look at the citywide dropout population. Through analyses of these data, OSSE obtained a clearer picture of the scope and profiles of the youth including demographic information, enrollment histories, and involvement in systems such as juvenile justice, foster care, welfare, and the homelessness continuum of care.

These data in turn informed the development of REC recruitment strategies, location options, and prioritization of specific agencies with which to develop initial recruitment pipelines. In the process, OSSE kept all student-level data confidential, and only provided access on a need-to-know basis to the city officials involved with the establishment of the REC.

The D.C. Alliance of Youth Advocates (DCAYA)—a local nonprofit and DYCN member—enhanced this research and data analysis by infusing the voices of youth themselves. With financial support from the Community Foundation for the National Capital Region and engaging the DYCN to design and administer surveys, DCAYA published *Connecting Youth to Opportunity: Better Understanding the Needs of Disconnected Young People in Washington, DC*[3] in October 2013. Capturing the voices of roughly five hundred current and former disconnected youth, the report defined key reconnection barriers, including financial, childcare, and transportation—findings that directly shaped the design of services for the REC to provide.

Informed and directed by this new body of local research, in summer 2013 the DME commissioned the National League of Cities' Institute for Youth, Education, and Families (NLC-IYEF) to execute a feasibility study for launching a reengagement center. Over the course of three months, NLC-IYEF surveyed DYCN members; interviewed local education, workforce, and human services agencies; conducted a scan of district resources and existing reconnection efforts; and—drawing upon the experiences across its national reengagement network—provided the district with a blueprint for startup.

KEY DESIGN FEATURES, TARGETED PARTNERSHIPS, AND THE MECHANICS OF STARTUP

Following DC's April 2014 Democratic primary election, the fate of the carefully laid groundwork to launch a reengagement center became uncertain. This uncertainty strengthened the resolve of city officials to open doors before the forthcoming change in mayoral administrations—only six months away. A triagency project team led the planning effort at this point, with each taking on distinct yet interrelated roles.

Office of the Deputy Mayor for Education (DME)

The Office of the Deputy Mayor for Education (DME) held responsibility for oversight and overall project management of the launch, including using the mayor's bully pulpit to facilitate cross-agency partnerships and resource allocation and providing seed funding.

Office of the State Superintendent for Education (OSSE)

The Office of the State Superintendent for Education (OSSE) took on the role of lead agency to manage the day-to-day operations of the REC. The feasibility study outlined the following management functions:[4]

- Hire and oversee a director to manage a minimum of two reengagement specialists, a data specialist, and day-to-day operations.

- Provide a staff reporting structure, with clear lines of authority and accountability within the REC and among partner agencies/organizations.
- Assemble, develop, and manage resources (public, private, and in-kind).
- Manage and share data.
- Oversee and evaluate effectiveness.
- Develop and implement a strategic expansion plan.

In addition to fulfilling these functions, OSSE uniquely held the ability to manage the REC in the city with its varied landscape of DCPS, independent public charter schools, and community-based educational options. As the State Education Agency, OSSE also maintained the most comprehensive set of local education and human services data for district students. These data equipped REC staff with critical information on individual enrollment status, academic history, and special education/English-Language Learner status as well as the ability to flag involvement in juvenile justice, foster care, and public welfare systems.

Moreover, OSSE managed local and federal grants to community-based nonprofit providers of adult basic education, GED preparation, and employment and postsecondary transition services. Lastly, OSSE had begun the process of driving forward statewide policy efforts to bolster the city's "second chance" system. With this broad citywide perspective of K–12, alternative, and adult programs across all three sectors, OSSE could operate an REC with sufficient neutrality to advise youth regarding placement options across a wide range of programs.

Department of Employment Services (DOES)

The Department of Employment Services (DOES) served as a key resource provider and programmatic partner, offering dedicated physical space within its newly renovated headquarters and providing two staff members in-kind to assist with REC startup. As the hub for the city's annual summer jobs program, DOES headquarters constituted a well-known location for tens of thousands of DC youth, provided a safe site in a high-need neighborhood, and stood adjacent to a busy bus depot and metro station serving multiple subway lines.

With roughly 25 percent of DCAYA survey respondents citing the need to work or lack of financial resources as barriers to completing high school, and more than a third reporting using DOES job services already, colocation allowed the REC to tap into an existing city resource in a way that would attract clients *and* offer immediate access to workforce-related services to address their needs.

Across these roles, the project team focused first on designing and developing the REC's core features, which consisted of the capacity to:

• Conduct targeted outreach to a defined list of youth ages sixteen to twenty-four without a high school credential (as well as engaging walk-ins and referrals).
• Assess academic status and nonacademic needs and use this information to develop individualized education plans.
• Identify good-fit educational options to attain a high school credential.
• Support the reenrollment process (e.g., collecting required documents, accompanying youth on site visits, connecting to resources that will address reconnection barriers).
• Provide ongoing support for at least one year after reenrollment.

In-kind contributions from across its three agencies helped the project team secure the inaugural REC staff team. The DME allocated startup funds to hire a director. DOES transitioned two of its Youth Program staff to serve as reengagement specialists. OSSE hired a senior-level staffer to provide reengagement services as well as strategic and data support. Together with the new REC staff, the project team then underwent a rapid development period consisting of several steps. These included:

1. *Initiate recruitment strategies, and shore up recruitment pipelines*: With access to home addresses (gathered through OSSE's data system), the REC executed a targeted mailing campaign. DME and OSSE also conducted training sessions for all youth-serving government agencies and organizations, and laid the groundwork for future colocated REC intake at various "hubs," including homeless services centers that assisted high volumes of families with heads of households ages twenty-four and younger and adult probation drop-in centers.
2. *Build a central, comprehensive knowledge base of current educational program options, in part by conducting site visits*: Reengagement specialists conducted site visits to roughly thirty potential education placement options, establishing relationships and becoming familiar with the individual sites' enrollment protocols and program offerings.
3. *Develop targeted partnerships to address key reconnection barriers*: DCAYA's youth survey data guided the project team to define barrier-remediation services essential at startup. Rather than requiring REC clients to travel to multiple locations to address financial, childcare, and transportation needs, the project team developed early relationships with core human services agencies to centralize these functions for REC clients. Partner agencies outfitted the REC to screen and

provide eligible clients with childcare vouchers, transportation subsi-
dies, job search support, and public welfare benefits on site.

The Role of the Disconnected Youth Change Network

Supporting the project team, the DYCN continued to provide a consistent
forum for cross-sector partners to convene and share feedback and guidance.
Pivoting from the earlier research support role, local Network members
formed ad hoc committees to provide program planning support for two key
startup needs: helping the DME and OSSE develop key position descriptions
and undertake a search for a REC executive director, and contributing their
cumulative decades of direct-service experience to inform the REC's intake
process.

Postlaunch, the DYCN remains engaged as the REC's Community Advisory Board, receiving monthly reports from the center's director and using its
convening power to address key challenges. The collective strength of the
DYCN has also revealed itself in the form of advocacy. Although the project
budget proposed to meet a majority of the REC's startup costs with in-kind
contributions from city agencies, the outgoing mayor's budget allocated new
dedicated local funds to expand staff and ensure sustainability in future
years.

The mayor submitted the budget under the careful scrutiny of the DC
council's Education Committee—whose chairman was running for mayor in
the November 2014 general election. Rallied by DCAYA, Network members
organized informational meetings with key councilmembers to educate them
on the need for and benefits of a REC, and testified at public hearings to
protect the proposed budget. In the end, the education committee went on to
approve the mayor's proposed budget, and even increased it by $100,000 to
permit hiring an additional eeengagement specialist.

POSTLAUNCH: SHIFTING FOCUS FROM STARTUP TO SUSTAINABILITY AND SUCCESS

In the months following the launch, DC stakeholders shifted their focus from
startup to addressing two key issues around sustainability: maintaining efforts across a transition in city leadership, and ensuring a sufficient overall
supply of return-to-school options.

Just two months after the REC ribbon cutting, DC found itself with a new
mayor, new deputy mayor for education, new state superintendent for education, and new chairman for the DC council's education committee. In the
early days of this leadership transition, key REC partners quickly organized
to meet with incoming officials and testified at agency performance oversight
hearings, advocating for staying the course. OSSE also hosted a series of

REC tours for new city officials and journalists, and launched a citywide multimedia ad campaign to keep up public interest and momentum.

DC's new mayor, Muriel Bowser, entered office determined to expand pathways to the middle class for residents and recognized that reconnecting young adults to educational programming is key to achieving this goal. Aligned with the mayor's priorities and understanding of the inherent value of the REC, the new deputy mayor for education and new state superintendent have continued to elevate reconnection as a top-level priority. The forward momentum of this work has continued with the hiring of two reengagement specialists since the launch. In addition, the new DC council education committee chair shares a keen interest in reengaging youth and has shown support of the REC's work.

Operationally, timely placement of students in best-fit options has cropped up as a key early challenge for REC staff, due to educational program capacity constraints and varied enrollment calendars. The ReEngagement Center only constitutes one piece of an overall reconnection system; ultimately, an insufficient supply of education placement options will greatly undermine the REC's efforts.

Now, with support from Raise DC, four key partner entities—the DME, OSSE, DCPS, and charter leaders—have begun to engage in a nascent effort to align and expand the landscape of options aimed at serving this population, driven by student age, credit, and skill-level data. With efforts such as these, and over time, the REC should come into its own as a force to assist the district in significantly honing its understanding of its dropout population, and in providing critical support in ways that increase opportunities for former dropouts' educational success.

NOTES

1. John Kingdon, *Agendas, Alternatives, and Public Policies* (New York: Longman, 2003).
2. Martha Ross, *Strengthening Educational and Career Pathways for D.C. Youth*, Metropolitan Policy Programs, Brookings, October 2011.
3. Anne Abbott, *Connecting Youth to Opportunity: Better Understanding the Needs of Disconnected Young People in Washington, DC*, The DC Alliance of Youth Advocates, October 2013.
4. National League of Cities Institute for Youth, Education and Families, Washington, DC Youth Reengagement Center Feasibility Study, September 2013.

Chapter Four

What Did It Take to Start Up in Allentown?

Jennifer Danese

One of the nation's newest reengagement programs took form over nine short months in 2014-15, in the rebuilding, formerly industrial, small city of Allentown, Pennsylvania. The story of the advent of systematic reengagement in Allentown features a partnership unique in the national landscape, fed by early commitment from local school district and workforce agency leaders. The story also suggests the benefits of seizing a particular moment in time and making highly effective use of prior examples from around the country.

TIMING IS EVERYTHING: LOCAL CONDITIONS AND DATA

Timing is everything. Whereas some advantages might have accrued from conducting a formal planning process including a robust feasibility study to establish reengagement in Allentown, moving quickly and seizing upon well-defined local interest and leadership brought even more weighty advantages. A lightning-bolt moment occurred in autumn 2014 when Dr. C. Russell Mayo, Allentown School District (ASD) superintendent, posed this question in a meeting focused on keeping students engaged in school: "What are we doing to serve students that have already dropped out?"

Dr. Mayo's question had its basis in key local data points. He and other leaders had seen the statistics that, for instance, 23.2 percent of adults in the city of Allentown under twenty-five years old do not have a high school diploma. In recent years, ASD had recorded dropout numbers of some four hundred to five hundred students per year. At any given time, the number of students between ages sixteen and twenty-two who have dropped out of school and still live in the city ranges from 2,400 to 3,000.

More broadly, the determination to move with haste grew out of the recognition that Allentown was and still is in a state of rebirth, revitalization, and growth. Thanks to the "Allentown renaissance," more people are increasingly frequenting the city center—complete with a newly erected state-of-the-art sporting event/concert venue and fresh, hip restaurants. Local leaders recognized that those people might only buy homes and stay in the area if convinced of the soundness of the local school district, and that a key part of the judgment of that soundness revolved around improved graduation rates and decreased dropout rates.

BACKGROUND ON THE CENTRAL OPERATING PARTNERSHIP

In Allentown's experience, a successful effort to launch an REC lies with and within a core strong, mutual partnership. Fortunately, the push for reengagement could draw support from a partnership between ASD and Communities in Schools of the Lehigh Valley (CIS), thirty years in the making. The rich relationship has featured steady growth in keeping with the noted high performance of the nationwide Communities in Schools dropout prevention model.

If it takes a village to raise a child, CIS raises the village, coordinating community efforts to support youth. Any child who has dropped out or has otherwise disengaged from school needs that support more than most. The mission of CIS is to surround students with a community of support, empowering them to stay in school and achieve in life.

In Allentown, CIS's role in a reengagement partnership stemmed from its long-standing area of emphasis on dropout prevention. Locally, this took the form of CIS's Graduate Allentown Initiative. The Initiative has the goal to increase graduation rates and decrease dropout rates by providing school-based, schoolwide supports, as well as case management for identified at-risk youth.

In the interest of strengthening prevention services, and relatively early in the implementation of the Initiative, ASD integrated a team of six CIS professionals into the district's two high schools in February 2015. ASD looked to CIS as a nonprofit leader with a proven success rate, as well as being the only dropout organization that can deploy an evidence-based Integrated Student Supports (ISS) model to yield strong results. On the prevention end of the spectrum, the CIS professionals working directly in the high schools aim to cut the dropout rate in half within five years.

A look at the local data and a reflection on the needs those data represented led the partnering team of ASD and CIS professionals to devise a second plank for the Initiative, so as to feature two elements: *intervention*—engaging disengaged and dropped-out students, to complement *prevention*—keeping current students engaged in school.

Adding a second plank involved rescoping the Initiative to embrace a newfound commitment to dropout recovery. This would stretch CIS beyond its most frequent realm of operations in the prevention sphere. Part of that rescoping involved bringing on the Lehigh Valley Workforce Development Board as a full third partner in order to meet returning students' needs for comprehensive career services, including marketable skill development and individual career planning.

PHASES OF PLANNING

Planning began in earnest as the partners established a joint vision for an Allentown ReEngagement Center (REC) to surround students with the necessary support to attain a high school diploma or GED, and to empower those students to realize and reach their greatest potential. The envisioned REC would target students who had already dropped out of school, or who might be enrolled but disengaged. Strong community outreach, a warm, personal invitation, and individual graduation plans would characterize the REC. The REC would provide students with support to launch out on multiple pathways to learning, in the form of a flexible range of options.

Assessment Phase

The planning team first wanted to learn the landscape of local and national efforts to support getting dropouts back to school to understand the successful options available for Allentown to adopt. ASD conducted an inventory of its programs and services. Key questions that the team considered included:

- What already exists in the district to support students in graduating from high school?
- Upon what funding streams do existing programs and services draw, and is the funding sustainable?
- Which of these district efforts are producing good results, according to data?
- What gaps exist?
- How can CIS support ASD in closing its gaps?

From his district leadership post, Dr. Mayo encouraged the team to seek answers to all these questions, while dreaming big.

The planners also ensured attention to student perspectives during the landscape assessment phase by conducting a survey of CIS alumni. The survey asked alumni questions, such as, What do you think are the most important factors to student success? What was the worst part of your school experience? Gaining feedback from the population to receive services and supports demonstrated value and respect.

CIS and ASD planners also gathered as much information and relevant research as possible. On this quest, seemingly endless questions emerged: Is anyone else working with dropouts? If so, who or what organizations are involved? Who leads the charge? Where do programs and centers operate nationally? What outreach strategies are available, and what works best? What successes and challenges do reengagement programs report? What do data on reengagement say?

Practical compilations of field experience, such as those published by the Rennie Center and National League of Cities, helped to answer many of these questions, or at least to point the team in the right direction. The Allentown planners also found it important to network and connect with others in the field. The nationwide Reengagement Network, although small and relatively young, provided an immediately available forum for learning from peers. For example, CIS accepted an invitation to the Reengagement Plus conference in Portland, Oregon, for December 2014.

The conference opened doors for additional networking with other attendees, such as the team from ReEngage Dubuque, Iowa. A subsequent conference call between the Allentown REC planning team and staff of the Dubuque program permitted delving deep into operational details. The planners also checked in regularly with the National League of Cities for additional referrals, and drew upon an online compilation of reengagement materials curated by NLC.

Adoption of a Planning Tool

The CIS and ASD team met regularly to share findings, best practices, and contacts, and they soon divided into subcommittees to address specific topics such as a timeline, operating space, funding, staffing, and data and documentation. Adopting and revising a planning tool that the Dubuque team had used in its startup stage proved particularly helpful in building a sound plan. The planning tool, embellished with the logos of the three partners as well as the graphically designed REC logo, detailed three core goals in a formal, written document.

Clarifying Goals

The team stated three main goals, as follows: goal 1: establish a REC for youth aged sixteen to twenty-four who drop out of ASD; goal 2: reengage 25 percent of students who drop out of ASD each school year; goal 3: develop individual plans for each dropout who reengages. Under each broad goal, the plan stipulates interventions and strategies (What action steps will staff take?), success indicators (What measurable results does the team expect?), assessment methods (How will staff collect data to measure progress toward meeting goals?), person responsible (Who will ensure the accomplishment of this goal?), and timeline (By when will the staff accomplish this goal?).

Assembling Sufficient Resources

With all parties invested in the planning process, the team addressed funding and resources for the REC. ASD committed to the role of major source of operating funds. CIS and the Workforce Board would in turn provide significant in-kind contributions, such as intellectual property, resources, existing staff time, facilities, and REC professionals.

Design Phase for REC Operations

With a sense of the landscape in hand, the team turned its attention to sketching an initial operating design that would meet needs and fill gaps. Key elements at this stage included:

Staffing. The planners' initial sketch included at least five full-time professionals; budget realities at the moment of startup ultimately resulted in scaling back this number with a view to expanding the staff of outreach workers as caseloads increase.

Student Flow. The team developed a flowchart depicting student movement through the REC, drawing upon flowcharts from other existing centers. The flowchart serves as a visual tool that represents the flow from dropout to diploma/GED attainment. It readily shows the alternative options available to students—home school placement, self-paced APEX learning, GAIN credit recovery, the proposed YouthBuild Allentown, and GED classes through Lehigh Carbon Community College—as well as functions that take place at the REC.

Roles and Responsibilities. Whereas all three partners contributed heavily to planning, they agreed on the need to establish clear roles at the point of implementation. CIS took responsibility for direct outreach, case management (intake, engagement, follow-up, and discharge), data collection and reporting, and fund-raising as needed. ASD agreed to provide financial support, space, in-kind building staff, access to student data, access to APEX accounts (for credit recovery), and counselor support for credit determination. The WIB committed to providing career intake and all career services.

Operating Policies. The plan also formally addresses many other topics with effects on operations. These included: physical space; memoranda of understanding; staff hiring; program management meetings; staff orientation; REC advertising at the school, district, and community levels; forms that the

REC will use to track and drive student success; the step-by-step REC process of intake/engagement/individual planning; and communication with partners and community organizations.

Development of a Staff Training and Individual Graduation Plan Template. As every student carries implications of his/her personal, familial, or societal role into the REC, the partners knew that support for individual students must address a range of nonacademic issues. These include homelessness, family disruption, drug and alcohol abuse, mental health, foster care, pregnancy, parenting, disabilities and abilities, low self-esteem, and more. With this in mind, planners took two steps: 1) designing staff training to surround students with a community of support, whether directly or through targeted community referrals; and 2) CIS created a tool called the Individual Graduation Plan based upon the tested CIS Student Support Plan (from the ISS in-school model), adapted to address the key elements of the REC process.

Professionals will complete each Individual Graduation Plan during a meaningful, empowering intake session to determine and record the student's academic and nonacademic needs. The Individual Graduation Plan becomes the vehicle of change for the student. The Individual Graduation Plan includes student demographics (such as age), risk factors, current course credits, career goals, and academic goals. It ensures that the student and staff remain on track for setting/reaching short-term and long-term goals while ensuring checkpoints at which to monitor progress.

Student-Oriented Branding. Further into the process, CIS surveyed another group of students to determine the REC colors and final version of the flyers, posters, and other materials. Finally, a local Allentown youth designed the REC logo.

Throughout the process leading to opening the REC doors with a program manager in July 2015 and outreach worker in August 2015, the planners from CIS, ASD, and the Workforce Board continuously sought out opportunities to communicate their shared vision with students, families, representatives of city and county government, and community partners so as to raise awareness and encourage support. Continuing to strengthen and broaden the local coalition supporting the REC remains a key task for the near future—so that, for instance, city government and additional community partners find ways to invest tangibly in the plan and the goal.

At this early stage of development of the Reengagement Network, the addition of a reengagement center in Allentown contributes palpably to the continuous evolution of the national landscape. Allentown looks forward to continued participation in the national Network, and to making contributions that ultimately generate proven best practices. Locally, as planning has given way to implementation, the partners consistently strive to optimize the success and operations of the REC—in part by maintaining communication with successfully established centers via phone conferences, site visits, and exchanges of data.

Chapter Five

Reengagement in Boston

Changing the Conversation and Driving Dropout Reduction

Kathy Hamilton, with Joseph McLaughlin, Matthew Mendoza, Lynne Powers, and Anika Van Eaton

Boston's high-profile dropout reduction initiative features one of the nation's first Reengagement Centers, developed in the context of a ten-year collaboration among the Boston Public Schools (BPS), the Boston Private Industry Council (PIC), and a range of public and nonprofit partners. Piloted in 2006 as two PIC outreach workers within a BPS program called Project Reconnect, the Boston Reengagement Center has reenrolled hundreds each year and served as a key driver of a 60 percent reduction in the Boston Public Schools (BPS) annual dropout rate.

Direct outreach to high school dropouts and Boston's multisector coalition have combined to mobilize and inform a major shift in focus toward out-of-school youth and struggling students. Education for all in Boston now means reengaging those who have left and those who are fading, not just those who attend regularly.

A commitment to continuous research complements Boston's community organizing and coalition-building approach, creating a tight loop between policy and practice. The interplay between research and action has driven a sequence of reforms that resulted in extraordinary progress. Among other effects, Boston's outreach effort made the need for a Reengagement Center (REC) to facilitate the reenrollment of returning students undeniable. The REC then generated compelling information that led to the additional reforms and capacity that Boston would need to sustain progress.

Through a cascade of direct and indirect effects, reengagement has proved critical to the dramatic decrease in the number of students dropping out of high school annually. This chapter will outline some of the measures of Boston's progress, discuss the dynamic interplay between the reengagement project and the coalition, and explain how the interplay drove the reduction of dropout rates and the increase in graduation rates.

THE IMPACT OF REENGAGEMENT: A NUANCED LOOK AT KEY DATA

The Boston Reengagement Center (REC) has directly reduced the number of disconnected youth in the community and helped hundreds of dropouts earn a high school diploma. As a result of the reengagement effort, Boston reframed the data measures used to consider the dropout crisis and progress in efforts to address it. By focusing on new measures that highlighted the trajectories of dropouts back into school, the initiative elevated dropout recovery as an essential part of addressing the urban dropout crisis.

Of note, the dropout reengagement project introduced four important new measures: the number of dropouts reengaged; the number of dropouts reenrolled in the district; the first-year persistence rate of reenrollees; and the graduation rate of reenrollees. Using these measures, it may help readers to review the scale of activity and effects. Over the past five years, since the REC opened, an average of 774 youth have visited the REC annually, with averages of 406 enrolling in a BPS school and 112 graduating each year. Since the beginning of the reengagement project in 2006, Boston has placed 2,335 disengaged youth within the Boston Public Schools.

The project hit upon a vein of untapped ambition among disconnected youth who wanted to advance themselves. Students such as Kendra Castillo have now graduated from high school and moved on to the next phase in their lives. Kendra says, "I think that the REC lowers the dropout rate because it opens a door that we close to ourselves when we leave school. The staff guided me to find a new school and encouraged me when I had a hard time going back. Now that I have graduated and I'm in college, I know that quitting my education was never really the option for me."

The number of reenrolled dropouts who eventually graduate shows the incredible potential of reengagement efforts. Over time, 762 of the 2,335 youth placed since 2006 have graduated. Most of the youth visiting the REC stand two or more years from graduation at the time of reenrollment, based upon credit accumulation, so it takes time to realize the ultimate outcome.

REC staff track each cohort over time to determine longer-term graduation rates. For example, during the 2012-13 school year, the REC placed 417 young people in a district educational program. By June 2015, three years later, 45 percent of them had earned a high school diploma. With reengaged students often facing significant academic challenges and time investment, this represents tremendous achievement. Additionally, hundreds more are still enrolled in school, with more than 70 percent persisting to finish their first year back to school—Boston calls this the "stick rate."

Since Boston first began organizing its dropout prevention and recovery coalition and its reengagement project, the city's annual (event) dropout count and rate has decreased from 1,936 and 9.4 percent in 2005-06, to 701 and 3.8 percent in 2013-14.[1] The REC even directly contributed to the decrease in Boston's annual number of dropouts because many—an average of forty-six per year over the last four years—were able to reenroll through the REC in the same year that they dropped out. See figure 5.1.

During the same time period, cohort graduation rates rose significantly as well. The four-year graduation rate in Boston increased from 57.9 percent to 66.7 percent between 2007—the first year Massachusetts published these measures—and 2014. The five-year rate also increased from 65.4 percent to 72.2 percent.

Cohort graduation rates are important for measuring school accountability. Indicators that provide quicker feedback are crucial to measure collective accountability. To track the impact of initiatives, the Boston coalition and dropout reengagement team use the annual dropout number and rate more

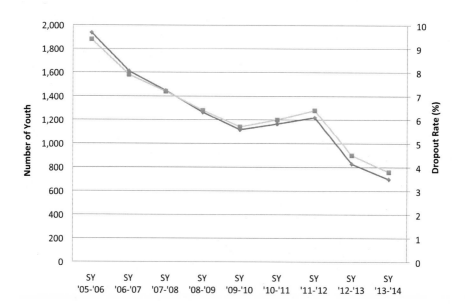

Figure 5.1.   Number of Dropouts and Dropout Rate *Source*: **Boston Public Schools**

frequently. Real numbers tell the story to scale, in human terms, while rates provide a reliable gauge of change over time.

The cohort graduation rate tracks first-time ninth-graders plus net transfers over a four-year and five-year period to yield a full picture of how many students from that cohort dropped out at any time over those longer time frames. In contrast, the annual dropout statistics track all dropouts from ninth to twelfth grade from the most recent school year. Therefore, the dropout statistics are more comprehensive in coverage.

In terms of broader implications, over time, this scale of dropout reengagement decreases the number of disconnected youth living in the community. A high school diploma represents a step forward for these young people. Without a high school credential or its equivalency, they face bleak economic prospects.[2] Boston has slowly reduced the proportion of dropouts in its sixteen-to-twenty-four-year-old population. Most recently in 2011 to 2013, the American Community Survey measured this group at 3.5 percent, down by nearly half from 6.1 percent in 2006 through 2008.

Synergy with the Coalition-Organizing Strategy

Boston's reengagement efforts and focus on new data measures crystalized the issues that the dropout reduction coalition sought to highlight, both driving change and making change feel more real. The urgency of baseline conditions and the progress along the way catalyzed school district and community partners to create a culture shift. This shift in turn led to new local policies that would benefit returning dropouts and prevent students from dropping out in the first place.

The coalition experienced a number of early wins that led to major changes. For example, a district study of those most likely to drop out led to the creation of a new credit recovery program and an early indicator warning system. The reengagement project drove home the need for these changes by bringing in young people who needed a changed approach, and making the young people visible.

Featuring the voices and faces of young people also provided the essential, human argument for the need for more and better alternative education options. The coalition got very little traction in that area until several years of reengagement showed that returning dropouts could succeed. Once decision makers realized that success was possible for those who seemed least likely to respond to intervention, they embraced the idea that it was worth the time and resources to address such students' needs—as well as the needs of students who were still in school.

A focus on reengagement also helped the coalition mobilize a growing focus on prevention in the district, and new protocols to ensure that prevention actually happened. To understand how this catalytic effect unfolded, it is helpful to understand the context in which Boston's reengagement project evolved.

ORIGINS OF THE COALITION AND REENGAGEMENT EFFORTS

In 2004, the Boston Private Industry Council (PIC) convened the Youth Transitions Task Force (YTTF), Boston's dropout reduction coalition. This coalition spent the first two years on research to create an environment where partners felt enfranchised to experiment with new approaches. The group believed that dynamic experimentation was necessary in order to spark policy changes. The Boston coalition represented one site in a national effort to lower local dropout rates, funded by the Youth Transitions Funders Group. Five cities developed strategic plans to address the dropout crisis, using data, leveraging each city's unique systemic context, and engaging the right mix of stakeholders and public leaders.

Boston's research included quantitative studies of dropouts and their socioeconomic prospects, qualitative research on the views of youth and parents in the community, and systems research on existing schools and youth programs. The coalition published this research and six core recommendations in a primer on the dropout crisis called "Too Big to Be Seen: The Invisible Dropout Crisis in Boston and America." These six recommendations included deeper and more accurate data analysis and early intervention and outreach to dropouts. The coalition actually believed that it was important to start with dropout reengagement in order to spark prevention.

GROWING MOMENTUM FOR DROPOUT REENGAGEMENT: BOSTON STRUCTURES ITS APPROACH

To jumpstart the action phase, the PIC tried a new approach, direct outreach to dropouts, while other coalition members tackled recommendations that fell within their areas of expertise. The PIC hired two young men who had once dropped out of high school themselves but had come back to complete high school and then college. These dropout recovery specialists were charged with reaching out to dropouts, learning their stories, and finding out what would happen when they were given a chance to go back to school.

The recovery specialists teamed up with Project Reconnect, a Boston Public Schools summer project that informed dropouts that they were able to return to school, joining the Project Reconnect guidance counselor in hopes of amplifying the project. The specialists used raw lists of dropouts provided by the school district to send mailings and make telephone calls to all those on the list.

That first year, the Recovery Specialists learned that students had to reenroll in the district at one of a number of Family Resource Centers (FRCs) around the city. As the sites of districtwide enrollment for *all* students, the FRCs were very busy, and the teenagers attempting to reenroll got frustrated. So, the specialists set up shop inside the FRCs to help the young people navigate, and the FRC staff welcomed their help.

From the beginning, these direct, staffed reengagement efforts interconnected in important ways with the YTTF's advocacy to make the case for change. The dropout recovery specialists presented their findings at monthly YTTF meetings, where district leaders and public and community agencies heard firsthand about these students who wanted to come back to school, despite all the obstacles returning students had experienced.

The team tracked and shared the reasons that students left school—a lack of connections to teachers and their peers, falling too far behind academically, and personal difficulties outside of school. This got educators and others thinking more specifically about the type of support that struggling students need.

In 2006, BPS commissioned the Parthenon Group and Jobs for the Future to identify the categories of Boston Public Schools students who were most likely to drop out. This groundbreaking study identified several groups: students who were older (over eighteen) and far from graduation, students who were younger (sixteen or seventeen) and far from graduation, and students who were older and close to graduation, as well as returning dropouts and teenage immigrants who had not yet learned English. [3]

By the time newly appointed superintendent Carol Johnson arrived in 2007, the coalition and the reengagement project had created momentum. Johnson immediately identified the dropout crisis as a priority and addressed it as a key aspect of her Acceleration Agenda, an overall improvement plan for the district, in 2008. This brought new district resources to bear on the issue.

In April 2009, district leaders opened the REC to increase the operating capacity of the project. From the outset, the REC has operated as a partnership between BPS, the PIC, and the YTTF. In addition to the recovery specialists, a BPS director with school leadership experience and a BPS guidance counselor rounded out the team, bringing instructional and administrative experience. The new team members helped REC provide more accurate guidance on schools and programs that would offer the best fit for reenrolling students.

THE ROLE OF DATA AT THE REC

The opening of the REC quickly accelerated the pace of reenrollment. Project Reconnect started by engaging 141 young people and reenrolling 72 in 2006 to 2007. At the end of the 2009-10 school year, the REC had engaged 550 and enrolled 301. By the end of 2011, the REC team had engaged 766 and reenrolled 430. See figure 5.2 for a depiction of changes over time, and placement into schools.

Because of the project's role in making the case for change, the REC staff team and partners placed a high premium on tracking program-level data. REC staff and district leaders learned from the project and made changes accordingly. The team built a fairly sophisticated Excel database and prioritized data entry and analysis among their responsibilities.

Subsequently, the PIC added a data analyst to the team to mine the data's research potential. Initially, this added position came in the form of a capacity-building VISTA, who joined the permanent staff after two years in the national service assignment. Among the many fields included in the database were demographics, school choice, school enrollment, academic progress, and graduation. REC staff analyzed and shared trends emerging from the database regularly with the YTTF, which in turn shared them with larger

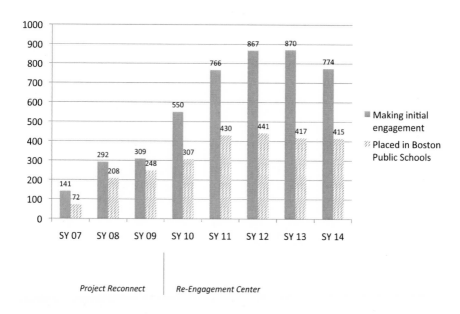

Figure 5.2.   Number Completing Reengagement Intake and Re-Enrolling in Boston Public Schools, by School Year

statewide forums organized through the Rennie Center for Education Research & Policy.

The numbers of dropouts returning to school each year had a profound cultural impact on the Boston Public Schools, youth-serving agencies, and the community. The sheer number returning each year demonstrated that these young people were worth investment. This bought important goodwill for both the young people and the cause. Local media coverage praised the project, and district leaders were proud to be leaders in innovation. In 2008, the Center for Labor Market Studies won the last doubters over by making the fiscal case for bringing back dropouts; the Center documented that the cost to Massachusetts taxpayers was $456,354 for each dropout over a lifetime.[4]

THE INTERPLAY BETWEEN REENGAGEMENT EFFORTS AND POLICY CHANGE

In Boston, visibility and the accompanying reframing resulted in policy changes. These included some relatively straightforward decisions to remove obvious administrative barriers to reenrollment. In the past, the district had automatically reenrolled dropouts in the school they had last attended. The reengagement project quickly revealed that few returning students wanted to revisit the site of a recent failure.

In response, district leaders changed the policy to allow reenrolling dropouts to choose a new school. Another policy change reduced the number of documents that returning students needed to prove residency to enroll. More profound policy shifts, such as a new focus on alternative options for reenrolling students, would require the sustained and coordinated efforts of the REC, the coalition, and partners.

Demand for Alternative Programs Drives School District Policy Responses

REC staff found a pattern in the school choice and persistence data. Reenrolling students preferred smaller alternative schools to larger traditional high schools, and stayed in the smaller schools at higher rates. Additionally, a high proportion of the returning dropouts were "old and far" from graduation. Boston has a thoughtful portfolio of targeted options for such students, with a number of district- and community-based options offering about 1,400 seats. However, demand among enrolled students was already high even before the REC opened, and once dropouts started reenrolling, the problem of available seats became acute. In 2015 alone, 480 REC students sought a seat in an alternative education program, but only 222 were placed.

The REC and the coalition worked together to highlight the need for alternative education, and the district responded by improving alternative program service delivery. The district worked with the coalition to develop a new weighted student funding formula that allows funds to follow students into alternative education programming.

The district also created the Boston Collaborative High School, a new constellation of community-based alternative programs organized into one administrative home school, with common graduation requirements, common professional development, and the opportunity to share resources. "Today, the ongoing data generated by the work of the REC is now a factor that will be helping to shape alternative program design and support interventions for students," says Ferdinand Fuentes, the executive director of Educational Options.

Much earlier, in 2008, the district took another important policy step by launching an online credit recovery program for the "old and close" students identified in the Parthenon study. The program was user friendly, and allowed students to make up credits by taking competency-based courses online. It proved wildly successful, starting with about 130 students and helping 350 to graduate in 2011 alone. A BPS study found that in 2012, this program contributed 4.8 percentage points to Boston's slowly increasing graduation rate,[5] and a university evaluation found that the program served BPS's most at-risk students.[6]

With a documented demand for alternative pathways and a long waiting list for school placements, the district allowed REC students access to the online credit recovery program in a classroom at the REC so they could make immediate academic progress while waiting to reenroll. The district embraced the REC's adaptation of credit recovery to serve a broader range of high-risk students, recently opening three new district credit recovery programs designed for returning dropouts and struggling students.

A Growing District Focus on Prevention

The REC also contributed to a new district focus on dropout prevention. Under Superintendent Johnson, the district trained school leaders, teachers, and school-based counselors to think about three tiers of risk and intervention. The district developed a "risk" indicator for high school students, using a research-based algorithm, which facilitated the tier system. This indicator is housed in the BPS database and is accessible by individual schools.

Traditional schools that enrolled a substantial number of REC referrals began targeting interventions, based on REC information about returning students' academic profiles. For instance, in the early days of dropout reengagement, Charlestown High School received a number of "old and far" REC students and already had enrolled a substantial number of these students. In response, school leaders developed Diploma Plus, a competency-based alternative program.

The Diploma Plus program director, Sung-Joon Pai, says, "When Charlestown High started enrolling dropouts referred through the REC, it really made us look at our students and our interventions. Ultimately, we realized that we had a lot of overage, undercredited students, and we designed our alternative program for these students. It has now been running for six years, and really does develop a sense of positive ownership in our students."

LOOKING AHEAD

Even accounting for the great progress that Boston has made on many fronts, important strides remain on the agenda in order to achieve the next substantial step-down reductions in the dropout problem. Increasing alternative education capacity—specifically targeted to the profile of students most in need—constitutes one area of emphasis. For this, the REC team and the YTTF plan to work closely with the school district on the development of the Boston Collaborative High School and other interventions.

Another goal involves developing postsecondary support connections. A recent PIC study of REC graduates indicated much lower levels of college engagement and persistence among REC graduates than among the full cohort of BPS graduates. For this reason, a recent project of Boston's Opportunity Youth Collaborative has been to open a Connection Center. The Center is based on the REC model but focused on subsequently disconnected high school *graduates*, including nontraditional graduates like those from the REC. The aim is to take the reengagement project to the next level by helping these young adults to gain access to college credentials, occupational skills training, and financial independence.

NOTES

1. "Q and A Boston Public Schools 2013–2014: Student Dropout Rates, 2014," Boston Public Schools Focus on Children, http://www.bostonpublicschools.org/cms/lib07/MA01906464/Centricity/Domain/238/Final Dropout1314.pdf.
2. Andrew Sum, Ishwar Khatiwada, and Joseph McLaughlin, *The Fiscal Economic Consequences of Dropping Out of High School* (Boston Private Industry Council, 2007).
3. Boston Public Schools, *Strategic Planning to Service Off-Track Youth*, Parthenon Group, September 2007.
4. Sum, Khatiwada, and McLaughlin, *Fiscal Economic Consequences.*
5. Boston Public Schools, *Impact of Credit Recovery Program on the 2012 4-Year Graduation Rate*, 2012.
6. UMass Donahue Institute, *Boston Public Schools 2010–2011 Credit Skills Recovery Program (CSRP) Key Research Findings*, 2012.

Chapter Six

Municipal Leadership for Reengagement

Andrew O. Moore

> When you take a person who is on the road to becoming a liability to the community—through increased reliance on social services and unemployment, for example—and you turn them around and make them a tax-paying asset to the community, that's a big plus for all of us.
>
> **—Dubuque, Iowa, mayor Roy D. Buol**

For many years, our nation's cities have stood at ground zero in the push to improve high school graduation rates. Despite recent hopeful signs, including a national graduation rate that reached 81.3 percent in 2013,[1] urban school districts continue to lag behind. *Building a Grad Nation*, a status report released annually by multiple organizations,[2] found that even in cities that have made improvements, graduation rates consistently hover between 60 and 70 percent.

Millions of young adults ages sixteen to twenty-four are not enrolled in school or have not finished their high school education. This education completion gap has enormous consequences for the economic health of our cities and the nation as a whole. The *Economic Value of Opportunity Youth*, a 2012 study by labor economists, estimated that each youth who is out of school and out of work "imposes—on average and compared to other youth—an immediate taxpayer burden of $13,900 per year and an immediate social burden of $37,450 per year (in 2011 dollars)."[3]

Research also shows that many out-of-school youth want to return to school but are uncertain how to do so and are fearful they will not succeed once they get there. Helping these young people find alternative pathways to graduation—and productive and promising futures—is a critical challenge facing municipal leaders today.

Fortunately, a growing number of cities now lead the way to solutions, with innovative strategies that provide multiple routes to graduation for all students. These efforts include the establishment of one-stop "reengagement centers" for high school dropouts. The centers offer a range of services such as individual academic assessments, opportunities to explore different education options, and referrals to appropriate schools or other credential programs.

As noted elsewhere in this volume, reengagement centers and programs can either operate in a central physical location or through roving staff or other "virtual" connections. Regardless of the specific approach, the goal of reengagement centers and programs is the same: to provide caring, well-trained staff that helps young people develop personalized plans to earn a high school diploma or GED.

An expanding national network of local reengagement centers generates numerous examples and ideas for city leaders considering how best to add reengagement to the local youth-serving infrastructure, and give young high school dropouts a chance to graduate and become productive members of their communities. The voices of two mayors closely involved with local reengagement strategies bracket this chapter, underscoring and exemplifying the opportunities for leadership.

LOCAL POLICY OVERVIEW

Municipal governments, as well as their state, federal, and school district partners, all have roles to play in providing a supportive policy framework for dropout reengagement. Several cities have taken the lead in assembling the funding and staffing needed to launch reengagement efforts. State governments, in their role as the principal locus for education policy, can establish incentives for school districts to participate in reengagement initiatives. Extending federal support to include dropout recovery as well as prevention helps underscore the importance of reengagement strategies in communities nationwide.

As with so many other areas in the education sphere, city leaders stand uniquely well positioned to raise the prominence of dropout reengagement as an issue, set public goals, and convene and sustain effective partnerships. As a complement to strong city leadership, support for reengagement can come in a variety of forms:

- *Partnerships* involving school districts and community organizations that contribute to youth development can play an integral role in reengaging dropouts. The reengagement program in Dubuque, Iowa, for instance, partners with the Community Foundation of Greater Dubuque's Project

HOPE, which facilitated the meetings that helped develop the Re-Engage Dubuque initiative.

• *School districts* can also take on the responsibility of establishing reengagement centers. For example, Portland (Oregon) Public Schools operates that city's Reconnection Center, and the Washoe County School District in Reno, Nevada, has operated as many as six reengagement centers.

• *Child welfare and other agencies* can play an important role in reengaging high school dropouts who are or should be in foster care. In Philadelphia, where a review of case files showed that more than 50 percent of dropouts had been involved with the child welfare system, the city's Department of Human Services worked with the school district of Philadelphia to establish and staff the city's reengagement center.

• *Private philanthropy* can provide startup funding or operating support for special projects such as creating data management capacity. In Omaha, for example, the Sherwood Foundation, initially in partnership with Building Bright Futures and the City of Omaha, provided seed funding for the Direction Diploma (D2) reengagement center.

Large cities may need to consider special adaptations. As described elsewhere in this volume, New York City's Department of Education established a multiservice center in each of the city's five boroughs. Philadelphia experimented with running a satellite reengagement center in a neighborhood with a high concentration of dropouts. Chicago positioned four reengagement centers in locations featuring high accessibility for large concentrations of dropouts. Los Angeles's Economic and Workforce Development Department set up new reengagement offices in sixteen youth centers throughout the city to help reengage one hundred thousand youth and young adults.

STRATEGIES MUNICIPAL LEADERS CAN EMPLOY

City leaders can employ a range of strategies to establish reengagement centers in their communities. Ideally, these centers would serve as the focal point of a far-reaching strategic effort to reconnect high school dropouts to good education and training options linked to the needs of the local economy. Five key leadership strategies emerge from field experience, as follows:

• *Highlight dropout reengagement as a necessary complement to dropout prevention.* Efforts to prevent students from dropping out have paid off in significantly improved graduation rates in recent years. Now it's time to focus attention on those who have already dropped out and may have fallen off the policy radar. The need is especially urgent in high-poverty urban areas where disconnected youth predominate.

- *Frame the size and growth of the "dropout pool" as a community problem—not simply a school district problem.* Put the weight of city government and the mayor's office behind a comprehensive strategy to reengage the "pool" of those who have dropped out. Long-term solutions will require a broad set of interventions and services that go well beyond the schoolhouse doors. Some may fall under the auspices of city and county government, and community groups may provide other services, such as mentoring programs and initiatives that combine education and job training.
- *Develop an effective messaging and communications strategy that keeps dropout reengagement in the public eye.* Mayoral speeches, events, progress reports, and the release of compelling data and success stories about young people benefitting from reengagement efforts can make an important difference. These approaches will engage the media and help keep the issue in the news cycle.
- *Focus dropout reengagement on preparation for the workforce as well as high school completion.* Efforts to help dropouts graduate from high school or earn a GED should include the next step—gaining a postsecondary credential that provides them with the skills to excel in the local labor market. For example, the Back on Track through College model, developed by Jobs for the Future, works with school districts, states, national youth-serving networks, intermediaries, and community colleges to reengage out-of-school young people by creating clear pathways to postsecondary education.
- *Embrace a cross-systems approach.* Pursue shared goals with juvenile justice, child welfare, and workforce development agencies. Each of these is likely to have ongoing contact with young people who need to reengage with school. Some may even be prepared to share the financial responsibilities of starting and operating a reengagement center.

ACTION STEPS: WAYS MUNICIPAL LEADERS CAN GET STARTED WITH REENGAGEMENT

Experience also suggests that city leaders can begin and sustain their support for a local push for reengagement through one or more of a series of action steps. The list below suggests a possible sequence for a city leader to consider.

1. *Conduct an inventory of local initiatives focused on dropout recovery.* City leaders do well to find out who in the community already takes proactive steps to reengage dropouts, perhaps through activities such as door-to-door outreach efforts, and who provides assessment and referrals to appropri-

ate high schools or alternative diploma programs. Local stakeholders will also need to collect information on existing education options, including what has been successful or challenging and what gaps exist. As part of this process, it may help to reach out to:

- Local school districts, which may operate alternative schools that serve high school dropouts
- Intermediate bodies such as county or state offices of education that work with multiple districts
- Individual charter schools specializing in enrolling formerly out-of-school youth, or organizations that manage networks of charter schools
- The local entity that oversees GED or adult basic education programs
- Community-based groups, such as youth development organizations that may work with dropouts

2. Take the lead in developing a dropout reengagement strategy. City leaders can use their convening power to bring together officials from the organizations mentioned above (school districts, intermediary education bodies, charter schools, and adult education and community groups) to formulate a reengagement strategy. In Washington, D.C., as described in greater detail in another chapter, the Office of the Deputy Mayor for Education commissioned a feasibility study for a citywide reengagement center. The deputy mayor's office used the ninety-day study process to consult with a range of stakeholders and city departments, and to test the feasibility of and support for the study's recommendations.

Elements of a successful dropout reengagement strategy likely include:

- An analysis of current offerings, gaps in services, and steps to address these gaps
- Recommendations on a coordinating entity or intermediary to lead reengagement efforts
- Suggestions for where to house the reengagement center
- Staffing options
- Recommendations on funding and sustainability, including opportunities for strategic city investment and realignment of existing spending

In some cases, city and school district leadership may come together to take advantage of funding opportunities and pool their resources to develop and implement a reengagement strategy. The City of Los Angeles Economic and Workforce Development Department (EWDD) initiated discussions with the Los Angeles Unified School District (LAUSD) to add a reengagement function to its existing network of thirteen YouthSource Centers already serving out-of-school youth between the ages of sixteen and twenty-four.

In this partnership, EWDD initially contributed $13 million to pay for physical space and to provide for operation of the centers by community-based organizations. EWDD raised an additional $12 million in the form of a grant from the federal Workforce Innovation Fund. This enabled the Youth-Source Centers to serve 1,200 more students and pay for rigorous evaluation. LAUSD placed a counselor at each of the centers to work with dropouts, representing an in-kind contribution totaling at least $1 million.

1. *Determine the most appropriate roles for city government in the establishment of a dropout reengagement initiative, including attention to strategic city investments.* Cities may get behind specific reengagement initiatives in various ways, including providing a physical location in unused city-owned space, having the mayor serve as a spokesperson, assigning staff to plan or direct the effort, or directing funding to specific aspects of the initiative. For instance, in Omaha, the mayor agreed to serve as the keynote speaker at a dropout reengagement summit, where he spoke passionately about the importance of helping young people reconnect with school. His speech occurred soon before Omaha's D2 Center for dropouts commenced operation, drawing attention to the center and its importance to the city.

   In both Omaha and Boston, city leaders have helped raise money for reengagement centers through private philanthropy. In Omaha, city funds have helped pay the salaries of the Youth Academic Navigators who work with the dropouts and monitor their progress. Philadelphia's assignment of child welfare staff to the city's reengagement center, and Los Angeles's repurposing of space at existing youth employment centers, constitute examples of strategic realignment of city budget resources.

2. *Establish an accountability system for reengagement efforts.* City leaders can play an ongoing role in monitoring the progress of reengagement centers, ensuring they are meeting critical goals and addressing barriers to success. A key component of this role involves working with stakeholders to determine what will serve as the agreed upon key indicators of success, and then developing a system for tracking and collecting data on those indicators. Members of the NLC Reengagement Network have adopted a common set of basic indicators. These indicators include:

- Number of young people contacted
- Number referred for services
- Number of students reenrolled and credits earned by those students
- The "stick rate," or percentage of students who remain in school through the academic year after they have reenrolled

- Percentages of students who have graduated or completed their GED, and who have progressed to postsecondary education

Cities may need to reconvene stakeholders on a regular basis to review this data and determine the best road forward to achieve sustainability. In its report on reengagement strategies in Boston,[4] the Rennie Center emphasized the importance of this accountability process in determining how the Boston Reengagement Center contributed to a threefold increase in the number of reengaged and reenrolled students. Such information, the report notes, not only helps pinpoint areas that need improvement, but it also helps reengagement centers compete for the funding needed to reconnect and otherwise support out-of-school youth effectively.

3. *Ensure continuous learning and improvement, especially during early implementation.* In addition to providing accountability on key indicators, city leaders should imbue local reengagement initiatives with a continuous improvement mind-set so that the efforts evolve as needed over time and learn from the experiences of other cities. Based on experiences to date, challenges city leaders should watch for include a shortage of high-quality alternative education placements for newly reengaged students, or a lack of readiness to accept students in alternative programs as the school year progresses.

The former suggests the need to identify means to expand alternative education; the latter, to provide more "open entry" options for students that are not tied to a semester calendar. Other potential challenges include the identification and training of specialized youth development–oriented staff.

FROM STRATEGIES AND ACTION STEPS THROUGH TO SIGNIFICANT LOCAL OPERATIONS

Two complementary examples from the Reengagement Network begin to illustrate the types of results a city leader could expect to see if she or he gets behind a new local reengagement initiative. Omaha provides an example of systematically arranging key supports to help youth navigate the path required to return to school and succeed. In turn, viewing Boston's experience through the lens of one student's experience conveys benefits at a very human level.

Omaha: Help to Navigate the System

In 2010, with Omaha's graduation rate hovering around 70 percent—nearly twenty points below the statewide average—a local partnership of the mayor's office and a nonprofit organization called Building Bright Futures launched the D2 Center, with funding from The Sherwood Foundation. The D2 Center (short for "Direction Diploma") connects dropouts and other disengaged youth ages fifteen to twenty-one to services in local school districts and alternative schools, such as credit recovery, online courses, and independent study. It also directly provides tutoring and elective credit classes for students who need alternative means to earn credits.

The center has reenrolled about two hundred students since 2011. Students primarily come with experience in, and may return to, Omaha Public Schools—Nebraska's largest urban district with about fifty-two thousand students in pre-K through twelfth grade. D2 staff assign each student a Youth Academic Navigator (YAN), who conducts weekly check-ins to ensure he or she stays on track. The center's four YANs also assist students on nonacademic issues, such as connecting them to resources in the community. Mayor Jean Stothert's office provides support in key areas, including a $50,000 grant for a YAN position.

Omaha took navigation as its theme after conducting a planning-period mapping survey of available reengagement services in the Omaha area. Following the multischool district, multipartner Multiple Pathways to Graduation Summit, the D2 Center's survey identified the range of options as well as important gaps. Gaps appeared in districts where summer school provided students the only option to recover missing credits. Capacity showed up in that some districts had already developed dual-credit programs with Metropolitan Community College and the University of Nebraska at Omaha.

Boston: One Student's Reengagement Journey

At the end of her junior year at Madison High School in May 2012, April Mae Smith decided that since she didn't have enough credits to graduate on time, and she didn't want to repeat her junior year, she would quit school altogether. April was among 1,219 students who dropped out of Boston public schools during the 2011 to 2012 school year, down from 1,936 in 2005-06.

April, who had been an honor roll student as a freshman but struggled to keep up her grades after joining the volleyball team sophomore year, briefly enrolled in Boston Public Schools' Re-Engagement Center (REC) to earn enough credits to become a senior in fall 2012. But her heart wasn't in it, and she quickly dropped out, moved to Rhode Island to be with her boyfriend, started doing drugs, became pregnant, and ended up homeless.

Soon though, April began looking for a way to turn things around so she could provide a better life for herself and her child. "I decided I wanted to graduate before my son was born," commented April at age nineteen.

When April decided to return to school, she again turned to the REC. Referred to the Boston Adult Technical Academy, April earned her diploma, and gave birth to her son, Jhaire, in June 2013. April subsequently enrolled in nursing school with assistance from REC staff. She credits the program with helping her get back on track. "The REC staff always told me if I needed help, to just ask," April says. "I learned a lot more there than what I would have learned in the classroom. When I graduated, I was one of the top students."

POSTSCRIPT: DENVER

Denver mayor Michael B. Hancock has actively championed collaborative efforts between city agencies and community-based partners to reengage out-of-school youth, and help reengaged students earn high school diplomas or GEDs. With hard work from Denver Public Schools, the city, and its part-ners, including Colorado Youth for a Change, Denver has cut its dropout rate nearly in half over the past five years to about two thousand students.

"That's still 2,000 too many," says Mayor Hancock. "Every day we wait to reach out to even one of those kids is a day when the overall health and economic well-being of our community—and the quality of life for these kids—suffers. If we don't develop a strategy to seek these youth out and create support systems that will lead them to success, then we are condemn-ing these young people to life as second-class citizens."

NOTES

1. EdFacts, "Regulatory Adjusted Cohort Graduation Rates," U.S. Department of Educa-tion, July 2012.

2. *Building a Grad Nation: Progress and Challenge in Ending the High School Dropout Epidemic*, America's Promise Alliance, Civic Enterprises, and Everyone Graduates Center at Johns Hopkins University, May 2015.

3. Clive Belfield, Henry Levin, and Rachel Rosen, *The Economic Value of Opportunity Youth*, Civic Enterprises, January 2012, 2.

4. Chad D'Entremont and Nina Zockoff, *Forgotten Youth: Re-Engaging Students through Dropout Recovery*, Rennie Center for Education Research & Policy, November 2012.

Chapter Seven

Waiting for Daniel

J. Weston Phippen[1]

At 6:30 a.m. Daniel Childs opens his eyes and lifts his head from bed with hopes to rise above what he calls his "consistency problem." The temperature outside is exactly freezing. Without a car, it will take the twenty-one-year-old more than an hour on the bus to reach his first week of GED orientation class, with transfers in the icy wind. The two-bedroom apartment he shares with an aunt and two cousins is silent. The room is dark. He is so far from what he hopes to become, and with change comes the possibility of failure. So many reasons to lie back down.

Two months ago, Childs walked into the D.C. ReEngagement Center searching for help. There, he found Dana Simpson, an intake counselor with a permanent smile who greeted him with a hug.

Childs told her he'd grown up in a rough, poor neighborhood. When he was still young, his father left—"just lost interest," Childs's mother puts it. Then his mom lost her job. Then they lost the family home. His little sister and mother moved into an apartment seven miles away, and Childs shuttled between friends and relatives. About this time, as he entered high school, Childs realized that the guys who wore the new shoes and fresh clothes didn't head off to punch time cards every morning. They stood in the streets all day—sold drugs or robbed homes.

Life out there seemed like the rap lyrics he'd grown up on. Childs joined them.

When Childs dropped out of school in 2008, about five million young men and women were considered "disconnected," in the category of sixteen-to-twenty-four-year-olds who neither attend school nor work. By 2011, after the recession, the number of disconnected youth had increased by more than eight hundred thousand.

The Riverside-San Bernardino area claims the highest percentage of disconnected youths, followed by Detroit, Charlotte, and Phoenix, according to
a 2013 study by Measure of America,[2] a project of the Social Science Research Council. In Washington, D.C., like many of those other cities, young
black and Latino youths drop out or are unemployed at rates two and three
times higher than their white counterparts.

As the country's minority population grows, this trend poses huge risks to
our global competitiveness. It threatens to immensely expand social spending—each disconnected youth costs $755,900 over a lifetime. And because
already one of every four young black men who drop out ends up behind
bars, it also threatens to condemn more black youths to prison.

President Obama has called this disconnection crisis both a "moral issue"
and "*the* economic issue of our time." Washington launched the ReEngagement Center in Autumn 2014 to address the crisis, with leaders calling it part
of the city's "second-chance system" for out-of-school youth. The questions
are the same, whether puzzled over by White House policymakers or ReEngagement staff members like Simpson: What drives this disconnection? And
how can we fix it?

At any one moment, the challenge can be as simple and as complicated as
getting one young man back on track to earn a high school equivalency
degree. Lately, when Childs pictured his future, he saw a telephone pole
wrapped in T-shirts that memorialized a murdered friend. He thought of a
deathbed promise to his father. So he spent the month of November getting a
new Social Security card and birth certificate to replace the old ones that had
been lost in numerous moves. In December, he found the ReEngagement
Center online.

The next day, he walked into Simpson's hug and told her, "I'm trying to
get into school." A placement test told him that while he excelled in writing,
he struggled with math, and because the center doesn't host classes, Simpson
drove him to GED programs around the city. Childs signed up for one in
Southeast, where a close friend of his happens to work. As Childs waited for
classes to begin, he spent nearly five days a week at the center, wary of
falling into old habits.

Up to six months of classes and tests in four subjects stood between
Childs and his GED. But the most immediate battle required that he show
up—every weekday morning, at 9:30 a.m., for three hours. First to a week of
orientation, followed by his first week of classes.

On this first day of orientation, as the clock nears 9, Simpson stands from
her chair at the ReEngagement Center. Childs had told her he'd meet her
before orientation. She glances at her phone. Childs has no cell.

Behind the ReEngagement Center runs the Anacostia River. To one side,
the neighborhoods are mostly white, populated by people with money, whose

kids had unrecognized advantages. To the other side of the river, black teens weigh survival against a seat in class.

For a few anxious moments, Simpson sits in her chair as her row of solar-powered bobbleheads nod back. She walks to the basement from the glass building's second floor, eases into a government sedan, and heads south on Minnesota Avenue. In the passenger seat rides a twenty-one-year-old mother named Bria Crawford.

Crawford dropped out of high school her senior year. She'd been expelled for fighting. She only needed a few credits to graduate, but her pride and embarrassment wouldn't allow her to transfer. Now she couldn't find a job, and she couldn't pay rent. Along with her two-year-old daughter, Crawford lives in a Quality Inn funded by the Virginia Williams Family Resource Center. A social worker there referred her to the ReEngagement Center, where Simpson asked what was stopping her from finishing her degree.

Small barriers often derail reenrollment, and since the ReEngagement Center opened in 2014 under the Office of the State Superintendent of Education, it has formed connections with citywide social services. When a young man or woman walks in, Simpson or one of her colleagues can direct them to housing, food, childcare, mental health services, and educational programs. The Covenant House in Southeast is one such resource, and after a fifteen-minute drive, Crawford and Simpson walk into the lobby.

As they do, Childs stands and says hello. He'd arrived thirty minutes early. Simpson says nothing, just smiles and hugs him. Then she leads Crawford down the hallway.

At 9:30, Childs unceremoniously walks up the stairs and into a classroom for orientation. Six students, all African American, sit at three rows of gray tables. Childs wears a puffy black coat over his tattooed arms and a beanie pulled down to his soft brown eyes. He signs the roll and sits in the middle. Arms on his lap, back straight, he looks ahead, where two teachers write the day's lecture on a whiteboard:

- conflict resolution
- conflict management
- dress code

"What's a recent conflict you got into, and how did you solve it?" one teacher asks.

The teacher glances at the three women in the room. "Come on, moms."

"I have problems every day," a young woman in the front row says.

"How about coping skills?" the other teacher asks. "How about just closing your eyes and going to that calm place?"

"My mind wanders too much," the woman says. "It's like a chatterbox. I wouldn't be able to just close my eyes. I be thinking about too much."

"OK," the teacher says. "What are the problems you had in other school settings that made you wind up here?"

"Skipping class," Childs offers. "You know, smoking, hanging out with the wrong crowd. Not doing schoolwork. Getting bad grades. Or it could be, like, something going on at home."

Childs's father left his nine-year-old son a love of rap, particularly of Tupac Shakur—and not much else. His mother was working as a special-education aide when she lost her job. Next went the home with the rose bushes his grandma had planted. Childs's mother and younger sister moved into an already crowded apartment with relatives. Childs moved in with his grandma.

He lived there for a year, and the two grew close, until he found his grandma dead on the floor from a heart attack. "He called crying and screaming," Martina King, his mother, says. He stayed with friends and relatives, and one day in class as a sophomore, Childs and his best friend, Saquan, got into a fight with a teacher. Together, they walked out of high school and into the streets. Childs turned to what he calls "the microwave life," where he believed money would come quick and easy, robbing homes or selling drugs.

His mother had finished high school, and that led to a life of hard work with little to show. To Childs, money was the problem. Also the solution. And the surest way to that seemed to be through music. The rappers he loved grew up like him. They wrote about a life like his. They had money.

Childs reconnected with his father just before he died of cancer. He promised to straighten up, yet he still thought of education as a means to support his way out through music.

He says none of this in class. It just balances atop those last words, "Something going on at home."

"Yeah," the teacher says. "Personal stuff."

After class, Childs sits in the lunchroom and spreads his feet wide. He leans back and his puffy coat reveals his sweatshirt, which he has had specially printed with the rap label he hopes to start: "Straight Up D.C." Below it are three letters: "G.M.C."

"Get Money Crew," he smiles.

The next day of orientation covers how to effectively communicate problems, then soft skills like workplace etiquette, then how the staff will distribute bus tokens. By Friday, Childs sits with his head in his hand while the teacher asks, "Tell me what it is you expect to get from Covenant House."

Employment, a student says. Financial stability, says another. Responsibility.

Childs has learned that Covenant House owns recording equipment, and already he has asked the staff to use it. When the teacher calls on Childs, he responds, "I just want to expand my music horizons." The teacher pauses.

"Also, I want to get better at math," he adds. The teacher writes it on the board.

Childs arrives early to the first day of class. At 9:30, the same six students take their chairs, and Childs again slides into the middle row. The teacher, an older white man, writes "a+b=c" on the board, for a lesson plan that will range from elementary math to algebra. "Don't be afraid to count out loud if you want to," the teacher tells everyone. "You might be embarrassed, but you'll be embarrassed with a GED."

After five minutes, a student walks out. A man in the back row slips in an earbud. A woman clears her throat. She spits into the garbage. She spits again. And again. "We'll also learn why in my time, they weren't called decimal numbers," the teacher says, pausing a bit for dramatic effect. "They were called Arabic numbers."

Childs leans his head against his hand. At 10:50, the class breaks. Only three students return to discuss decimals and fractions, and by 11:20 every-one but Childs has vanished. Now the teacher lectures about the Moorish conquest of Spain, then something about Alexander the Great and the Mon-gols. Finally, the lesson weaves back to numbers. "So we call everything between zero and nine a digit, because what's another name for fingers?" the teacher poses to the class, which is Childs. "And how many fingers do you have?"

"Ten," Childs answers.

"Exactly."

Childs walks downstairs and slumps into a seat in the lunchroom, an extension of the lobby with six round tables and vending machines. His childhood friend, Saquan, whom he dropped out of school with and who now works at Covenant House, walks near with a laptop.

Saquan opens the laptop and scrolls through a list of their songs, recorded in his homemade studio. Some of the titles read, "Club Shit," "Out the Mud," and another that begins, "Time to get this money . . . money, money, mon-ey . . . " As the track winds up, Childs raps along and bobs in the chair.

Three other men hear the music and join the table. Partly bragging, Sa-quan tells them he's exhausted because Childs and another guy were at his house all night in his studio. "You seeing me here?" Saquan asks the student. "I be drained. They do nothing but rap. That's all they do."

"'Cause we trying to get *rich*," Childs says from over his shoulder.

"And they don't want me to get no sleep," Saquan says. "They say, 'Man, what you doing?' I say, 'I got to go to work in the morning.'"

Saquan, twenty-one, earned his GED a little more than a year ago. He first came to Covenant House for job training. "He was extremely raw," says Cliff Rogers, who coordinates Covenant's work-readiness program. "No employ-ment. No résumé. No soft skills."

Rogers helped Saquan get his first job bagging groceries. A few days later, Saquan wanted to quit. It was too far; he disliked his coworkers. Rogers told him no, first he had to find another job. Saquan ground it out until he found one, and later when he complained about that job, Rogers stayed on him until he found another. He eventually became the first former student hired full time at Covenant House, where he answers phones and cleans the building.

"Now he's really understanding that work is a commitment," Rogers says.

The music rolls into a chorus.

Childs's first day of school had felt nothing like rap lyrics. It had not been quick and easy. The students sit around the table, and the chorus sounds like a mantra. "GMC, GMC we up now . . . "

On Tuesday, Childs again arrives early. On Wednesday, three students learn how to solve for "x." Childs is not one of them. He doesn't show the next day, either. On Friday, still no Childs.

The gap is, and is not, about race. In scholarly papers, the gap is about poor neighborhoods and residential segregation. Housing prices push lower-income families away from employment areas and into neighborhoods that lack effective public transportation. This creates islands where unemployment is common, higher education is scarce, and poverty is standard.

Russell Krumnow, managing director of Opportunity Nation, says in America we'd all like to believe that a person can come from nothing and rise to the top, that success is about the individual. But the reality is that "circumstances and zip code of birth have way too much impact on how high you can climb on that ladder of opportunity."

The gap is largely about poverty, and black communities across America face double the poverty rates of whites, double the unemployment.

On the ground floor, to Saquan, that looks like this: "Think about this, you're around 10 people, and everybody goes to college—you're going to be inspired to go to college, right? If you're around 50 people, and 10 sell drugs, 15 rob, 10 locked up, and [the others] don't do nothing but smoke all day, where is the inspiration coming from? And when you see mom struggling, first thing you think is, 'Let me get some quick money so she won't struggle for the moment.'"

"I was taught to take care and provide," he says. "That's it. To make sure your mother is good, your brother is good, sister is good, and your little cousins. So my safety was never really my concern. As long as I survived enough to make sure that they're good, to see them grow up—fuck my life. That's how I carried it. And just now, I'm really starting to realize how valuable life is."

Simpson hears nothing from Childs all week. Meanwhile, lawyers bring their young clients into the center; a staff member speaks to law-enforcement agencies around the city. Into the center walk single mothers, shy young men, teens with anger issues, the homeless, and those from broken homes. Nearly all are black. Nearly all from one side of the river.

On Thursday of the second week, Childs again walks into Covenant House. Rogers, the manager, pulls him aside. Where has he been? Rogers asks. Why didn't he at least call? Childs says he was sick. He had no phone. Nobody's number. And when he got better, he'd spent a few late nights working on music and was too tired.

Change is a process, and Rogers knows this. Any time you ask a person to rearrange their habits, it'll be difficult. How often has Childs's own life ever been consistent? How often has it been dependable? Childs leaves the office for a seat in class.

The following Friday, Childs takes a bus from Covenant House to the ReEngagement Center, as he has not seen Simpson in three weeks. He boards the bus with Crawford, the woman who rode with Simpson on Childs's first day of orientation. They sit beside each other, not saying much at first. Crawford asks if he has used the Covenant House recording equipment yet.

"No," Childs says. "I was going to, but Mr. Rogers said I got to focus on my school work."

"Yeah," Crawford says, staring out the window.

"I'm trying to get all this going," Childs says. "It's just—it's going to take time, you know?"

NOTES

1. This chapter first was first published as an article ("Waiting for Daniel: The Slow Journey from the D.C. Streets") in the April 1, 2015, edition of *The Next America*, a section of *National Journal*.

2. Sarah Burd-Sharps and Kristen Lewis, *Halve the Gap by 2030: Youth Disconnection in America's Cities*, Measure of America of the Social Science Research Council, October 2013.

II

Important Techniques in Reengagement

Chapter Eight

Eight Promising Outreach Strategies for Reengagement

Steve Dobo and Shirley Horstman

Outreach efforts to students who have left high school before graduating have flourished and matured over the last decade across the country, so that by now, practitioners have tried and explored many new methods. Some outreach strategies involve developing strong working relationships with community-based organizations and local school districts. Others involve hiring staff who can find, surface, and intercept these students in the parks and malls that they so often frequent.

Recent evolutions in outreach utilize technology and social media to leverage scarce staffing resources. Still others continue to use the tried-and-true methods of calling students based on school district student contact information, and leveraging contacts with these students to find other students through peer referrals.

No matter how reengagement programs reach out to young people—and the list of ways continues to grow—one key consistent theme emerges: getting directly in front of young people (physically or virtually) who have left school, and quickly building trust and strong relationships to present them with viable school options and a supportive process that helps them reengage in school.

With this theme in mind, this chapter discusses the top eight promising outreach strategies, based primarily on experience in several Colorado school districts and in Dubuque, Iowa. The eight strategies, few if any of which are mutually exclusive, include outreach specialists, marketing, social media, technology, canvassing, high school partnerships, community-based organizations, and peer referral.

OUTREACH SPECIALISTS

Dropout reengagement via outreach specialists got its start in Boston with the Boston Private Industry Council–Boston Public Schools partnership, and in Denver with Colorado Youth for a Change (CYC) partnerships with local school districts. Boston Public Schools and Denver Public Schools agreed to provide student-level contact information, usually in the form of a list of dropouts generated from district student information systems, which sometimes extended to direct access to those systems. The Boston Re-Engagement Center and CYC used that information to contact dropped-out students from the school district.

These organizations hired outreach specialists, often with backgrounds similar to dropped-out students, to call students and build relationships with them in order to help them return to school. Several years later, Re-Engage Dubuque adopted the outreach specialist strategy in a smaller-city context. Dubuque's deployed staff specialists conduct home visits in order to jump-start the relationship when a student is not responding to phone calls.

In both Denver and Dubuque, the outreach specialists become experts at recommending the "best fit" for a return-to-school option by learning about the offerings and culture of all the possible schools and programs in which returning students could enroll. Often, outreach specialists provide students with several school choices that could constitute good fits, and take students to the school to meet school staff and other students to gather information to help make the school decision.

Once the student makes a return-to-school choice, the specialist will often help the student fill out the paperwork to reenroll in school. Along the way of getting enrolled in school, this supportive adult helps students address any barriers they have in returning to school, such as transportation, work, childcare, and academic deficits. When school district student contact information is available, this strategy is by far the most effective in the reengagement outreach toolkit.

Textbox 8.1
Suggestions from Zero Dropouts Regarding Outreach Specialists
Expectations:

- Attempts to contact eight hundred to one thousand out-of-school youth per year, case manages one hundred of these to get sixty-five back in school, and provides follow-up services for the ensuing year.
- For any given list of previously uncontacted dropouts provided by a school district, get 12 percent of students on that list back into school.

Qualifications:

- Successful experience overcoming adversity, preferably educational adversity.
- Bachelor's degree in psychology, sociology, education.
- Experience as an educator, no longer interested in classroom role.
- Professional or extracurricular background in ethnic studies, social justice, or similar.
- Match the population they serve in terms of ethnicity.
- Young at heart.
- Good at developing trust quickly with youth.
- Believe that all youth can succeed.

Topics on which to train:

- Navigating student information systems.
- Interpreting transcripts.
- Conducting effective visits and research on alternative school options.
- Developing relationships with key hand-off staff at each option.
- Intake and assessment procedures.
- Data input into database.
- Wraparound supports available in the community for transportation, mental health, substance use, homelessness, jobs, job training.
- Opportunity to shadow a more experienced outreach specialist for several days.

Support Mechanisms:

- Weekly case management meetings to discuss where students stand along the pipeline.
- Weekly staff meetings of outreach specialists.

MARKETING AND PUBLICITY

A second strategy involves publicizing available reengagement services and supports. The extent of marketing publicity that a reengagement program requires depends on the demographics of the targeted area and the density of the population targeted for reengagement. Whether in a large community such as Denver or a smaller city such as Dubuque, reengagement programs will likely find local media outlets and partners eager to help spread the reengagement message by combining a variety of no-cost or inexpensive traditional and more creative approaches.

In Dubuque, the local newspaper looks for human interest as well as news stories, and will research and run stories on students who have overcome significant barriers in their lives to graduate. In one case, when such a story appeared, several residents reached out to the reengagement coaches and asked them to contact their children, grandchildren, friends, and neighbors who had dropped out of school.

Denver's reengagement marketing effort has involved billboards, banners on public transit systems, and public service announcements, and found all effective as ways to generate interest. To complement the broad communication tools, Denver has at times employed more individualized strategies, including door hangers, direct mailing, and communications from community-based organizations.

Denver and Dubuque have both found Facebook and other social media sites to provide inexpensive ways to reach youth. Some schools and organizations have done Saturday sweeps of neighborhoods to invite disengaged youth back to school.

A key marketing tool involves fielding outreach specialists, sometimes called reengagement coaches, who consistently establish appropriately supportive relationships with youth. These specialists transmit the belief that each student they work with has the ability to reach his or her goals. Experience has shown that the "never give up" attitude of the coach spreads contagiously, and also leads to peer referrals.

SOCIAL MEDIA

Successfully reaching disengaged young adults continues to prove challenging, and requires constantly shifting and adapting strategies. For the last several years at least, what remains constant is the evolution of new forms of social media, and the faithful following of these shifts by technology-savvy youth. Thus, several reengagement efforts have determined the need to communicate through a wide variety of social media tools in order to reach the targeted audience.

- Facebook provides an easy way to post messages. Individual reengagement coaches can easily establish a unique "reengage page" for almost instant communication with youth, even when the coaches have little other contact information for the youth.
- Since so many young adults have smartphones and few will answer an unknown phone call (or known for that matter), texting provides another effective contact strategy. Youth behave as though intrigued by receiving

a text, and will usually respond if only to ask, "Who are you and what do you want?" Texts also serve as a tool to remind youth of reengagement appointments or other important meetings as well as relationship-building messages such as happy birthday well wishes.

- Twitter provides another tool that some coaches and youth find appealing. Entire conversations can unfold during tweets, and coaches can use Twitter to inform followers about services, program statistics, and in general give constant reminders of the programs available to followers.
- Coaches and students can use Snapchat to send quick "See you in ten minutes" messages or other types of short communications. Instagram delivers the ability to record and immediately post a quick photo or video on Facebook, Twitter, or other sites such as Tumblr.

Textbox 8.2 Sample Coach-Youth Social Media Interaction: Dubuque
Coach: Hey Sarah. Get in touch when you get a chance. This is your coach, Temwa.
Student: Coach for what? IDK who the hell you are, leave me alone. I obviously deleted you for a reason.
Coach: I work for the Dubuque Community School District. I am a reengagement coach. I work with students sixteen to twenty-one years old. It's your call if you want to pass up the opportunity we wanted to talk to you about. Let me know.
Student: OMG I'm so sorry!
Coach: LOL it's OK.

WEB-BASED DIGITAL TECHNOLOGY

When considering the sustainability and scalability of reengagement programs, World Wide Web–based digital technology offers a lot of promise to minimize program costs. At-risk youth require a great deal of personal attention, which caring and knowledgeable staff members deliver in both Denver and Dubuque. Experience to date suggests that the need for human contact with reengagement specialists will never go away. However, the creative use of digital-based outreach can often extend the range of these personnel.

For instance, the community-based organization Zero Dropouts created "Drop in Denver" campaigns in 2013 as a student intercept approach to utilize creative guerrilla marketing techniques via the innovative technology of virtual coaches. The campaigns blanketed the city with flyers, stickers, posters, and billboards, all with the message "Denver wants dropped-out students to come back to finish high school." Students could text, call, email, or visit a website featuring a virtual counselor who encouraged out-of-school students to return to school.

Denver's mayor, Michael Hancock, served as the spokesperson for the campaign; he recorded a thirty-second public service announcement that ran on the local television station. Once on the website, students, family members, educators, and concerned citizens could find information on the dropout crisis and get connected to an outreach specialist to help any young person return to school.

Encapsulated proof of concept appeared through the example of a young woman whose boyfriend saw a Drop in Denver poster when they got off the roller coaster at the Elitch Gardens amusement park. The boyfriend said, "That's for you." They made contact by text, and within two weeks she started a GED program.

In similar ways, reengagement campaign organizers have employed digital technology to broadcast "smart stories" by email and text to dropped-out students and concerned adults in those youth's lives. These "Reset Your Life" smart stories utilize an informative and engaging approach to share information about returning to school, and also to encourage students that they can return and finish high school. The latest technology even allows the student to become part of the smart story, with his or her name included on a high school diploma floating across the virtual scene.

CANVASSING

Especially in cases in which reengagement programs do not have access to student-level contact information, an effective strategy remains available: canvassing. Canvassing involves hiring a team to conduct street outreach in order to surface and intercept young people who have dropped out of school. Canvassing's effectiveness proved out in Southern California in the summer of 2014, when twenty-five outreach specialists with Zero Dropouts found 450 students in three months to return to school.

Canvassing team tactics typically begin with identification of "hot spots," at which canvassers can find a consistently large number of people who seem approachable. These hot-spot areas include city parks, outdoor and indoor malls, bus and light rail stops, courts, admission lines for music venues, and community events.

A related form of canvassing involves setting up a table, kiosk, or sandwich board at a community event in order to distribute information and engage in conversations with young people or others who might know young people who need to get back into school. In such settings, having canvassers wear matching T-shirts with program logos or messages about education helps bring cohesiveness to the effort and attracts attention. Other canvassing efforts have involved going door to door to engage in conversations and leave promotional literature; over time these efforts have proven to be less successful than meeting people in public places.

Three top priorities emerge across all types of canvassing efforts. Canvassers must immediately build trust and a relationship with the young person, present information clearly using a flyer or similar means, and gather the young person's name and cell phone number. Some street team members immediately text or call the number while standing with the student to ensure that it is a working number and that they have a solid connection to the student. Another necessity: immediate follow-up, for contacts made on the street grow cold quickly if not nurtured through follow-up conversations and visits to the school.

HIGH SCHOOL PARTNERSHIPS

Taking a broad view of the potential reengagement population to encompass struggling students as well as those who have already left school, local high schools can serve as essential partners. High schools with attuned personnel and systems can readily identify students who are in the process of dropping out of school, and oftentimes shore up a caring adult relationship to launch the process of finding a school that provides a better fit. Scooping up students early, as they waver on the edge of dropping out, renders moot the often more difficult processes of trying to locate the young person post dropout, gaining access to student information systems, and more.

Some high school personnel have good relationships with young people and can help bridge those relationships to productive relationships with an outreach specialist who can help find a new placement. Later, at the time of student reenrollment into a new school, cultivated staff member-to-outreach specialist relationships prove essential to ensure a warm handoff to a caring adult. For example, Re-Engage Dubuque screens potential coaches carefully for the ability to form healthy, meaningful relationships with at-risk youth *and* school personnel.

COMMUNITY-BASED ORGANIZATIONS PARTNERSHIPS AND REFERRALS

Community-based organizations, such as nonprofit organizations and churches, provide another channel to find students who have dropped out of school. At one end of the continuum, some school districts in Denver and neighboring communities contract with the nonprofit organization Colorado Youth for a Change, tapping into CYC's mission and expertise to solve the dropout crisis and find and help dropped-out students return to school.

Another choice involves contacting and building referral relationships with community-based organizations with expertise in youth development and ongoing contact with significant numbers of young people. In Denver, Dubuque, and other cities, reengagement programs have successfully engaged YMCAs, Boys and Girls Clubs, youth homeless organizations, city recreation centers, and youth leadership organizations to surface and reconnect at-risk youth.

Organizational relationship building involves steps such as having outreach specialists attend the staff meetings of these organizations to share information about school programs and processes for gaining access to reengagement services. Specialists leave flyers behind with staff members who work with young people, follow up regularly to encourage and receive any student referrals, and often meet with prospective students on site at the community organization. This approach works especially well when no need exists to find students quickly for the start of a school year. These interorganization relationships have their basis in trust building and nurturance through responsive interactions over time.

PEER REFERRAL

Peer referral constitutes another powerful tool to reengage young people in education. Typically, students slowly disengage from their schools and begin to skip classes to hang out with friends. Because of this dynamic, Re-Engage Dubuque quickly learned that finding one student who has dropped out of school frequently leads to finding a group of friends who have also dropped out from school.

Experience shows that the majority of disengaged students do not want to be considered "dropouts" and really do want to finish their high school diploma or get their GED. One such student may respond well to outreach and the investment of considerable time to help reach goals. Success with one student who overcomes numerous barriers brings hope and encouragement to others. As programs mature, students who have achieved success after reengaging may even progress into roles as coaches, and can reach out to additional families and neighbors.

Textbox 8.3 Peer Referral Example

Coach: We need to set up a time with the community college to get you testing next week. Monday @ 1 usually is their open day. Have you already tested? I forget. Are you also looking for a job?

Danny: No not tested yet n yes still looking

Coach: Gotcha. I'll schedule something Monday at 1. Does that work for you?

Danny: ok and my friend 2
Coach: That's fine. I'll call and get that set up and let you know. What's their full name?
Danny: Diamond **** she went 2 senior
Coach: Gotcha. I sent a friend request to her you're both on for Monday @ 1.
Danny: ok thank u

Across the nation, members of the Reengagement Network have employed a variety of different outreach approaches and strategies drawn from the list of eight above. Whether or not a reengagement program can obtain access to student-level contact information through a partnership with the local school district marks a key bifurcation point in determining which strategies to utilize. School-level information provides immediate access to identify dropped-out students and phone numbers to reach them directly or by means of a nearby adult.

Without that information, reengagement programs have adapted creatively by utilizing technology and social media, along with canvassing and innovative marketing campaigns to surface young people who have dropped out of school. In either case, once a student has received assistance to return to school, she or he often represents one of the best routes to reach other students through peer referral. Whereas outreach strategies have come a long way in the past decade, in order for the strategies to remain effective, the methods will need to continue to adapt to the constantly changing styles of communication of young people.

Chapter Nine

"A Student Is Much More Than a Number": Using Data to Improve Reengagement in New York City

Alexander Thome

New York City operates a massive school district with many options for high-school-age students to earn their diploma. In total, across the age span, over 1,800 schools enroll more than 1.1 million students. In addition to a large group of high schools for on-track students, the NYC Department of Education (DOE) also offers a portfolio of schools and programs for students who struggled in the traditional high school setting. For instance, such students may enroll at "transfer schools" if they have dropped out or fallen behind to earn credits to graduate and develop college and careers plans for life after high school.

In addition, Young Adult Borough Centers (YABCs) offer evening classes four nights a week for credit recovery and prep for New York State's exit exams. Students with children may use free childcare in schools provided by the DOE. Also, notably, the DOE offers a large high school equivalency prep program called Pathways to Graduation. Yet even in such a big city with so many options, some students get lost or drop out.

Thus, Referral Centers for High School Alternatives, managed by the superintendent of alternative high schools and programs, operate in each of the city's five boroughs, with the common mission to offer students and their families a place to meet with an expert to discuss all options for resuming education. Staff at the Centers encourage students to continue their education, help guide their next steps, and then advocate on their behalf. In a system as big as New York's, offering expertly staffed, geographically accessible Centers provides an invaluable resource for several groups.

Beneficiaries include students and families; school counselors with large caseloads; community-based organizations supporting individuals; and individuals who want a little support to figure out their educational path. Nearly eight thousand students visit Referral Centers each year for guidance, and the Centers' collective goal is to place as many as possible back in school. This requires extreme persistence and attention to the demands created by the large scale.

To this end, Center staff and administrators have experimented with many changes over the last several years, from facilities improvements and reworked staff models to trainings and technology improvements. Driving many of these experiments: close analysis of student data. This chapter discusses how New York's use of data informed two key aspects of student reengagement efforts, determining the most effective means of outreach to get prospective students into the Referral Centers, and getting students reenrolled in an educational option.

Examining and tailoring outreach involved more intensive use of geographic information systems and tracking the effects of various outreach techniques. Focusing on enrollment, by contrast, involved disaggregating school placement information and following up based on findings.

GETTING STUDENTS INTO THE REFERRAL CENTERS

Historically, the Referral Centers have not carried out extensive outreach and recruitment—word of mouth kept the Centers busy enough. Also, because Referral Centers have the function of enrolling students in the Pathways to Graduation high school equivalency prep program, any student looking for that service makes a visit, contributing to a relatively high volume of visitors.

And yet, over the last couple years, the Centers witnessed a decline in visitors needing reengagement or high school equivalency prep enrollment assistance. In contrast to the falling traffic levels at the Centers, the prospective demand for alternative programs remains high. Best estimates show nearly fifteen thousand students under the age of twenty-one dropped out of NYC schools during the 2013 to 2014 school year.

Finding Students Who Dropped Out

Given the prospective demand and declining visitation, staff of the Centers set out to find the candidates for reengagement, using data to drive and guide a newfound commitment to outreach. Drawing upon the DOE central office data systems, managers generated a list of the students who had dropped out over the last year and were younger than twenty-one years old. Using students' last known addresses (and Tableau software), the DOE team could readily see locations and concentrations of students who had dropped out.

This look in turn helped in targeting outreach efforts to neighborhoods with higher proportions of students dropping out.

Further cuts of the data along geographical lines permitted an examination of rates of visitation to Referral Centers. This helped the team understand where it already experienced a reasonable level of success in welcoming students into a Center, and which neighborhoods offered opportunities to increase visitation rates. Figure 9.1 helps to visualize this information by showing which of the students that dropped out last year had visited a Referral Center.

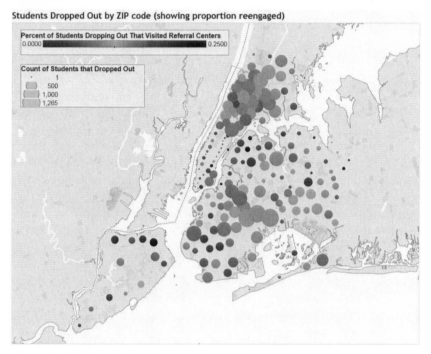

Students Dropped Out by ZIP code (showing proportion reengaged)

Figure 9.1.   Students Dropped Out by Zip code (showing proportion reengaged)

Reaching Students Who Dropped Out

Looking at the data in these ways helped the NYC team identify where they could expect to find the students that they wanted to reach. Thus began the harder work of outreach. Over a one-year period, the team tried a very broad approach with mixed success.

Employing what Dobo and Horstman (chapter 8) refer to as marketing and publicity techniques, the Centers generated posters and palm cards to post and hand out in the target neighborhoods. Staff asked local delis and bodegas to post the signs. Staff also visited community centers and other city agency offices to introduce the Pathways to Graduation program, and left palm cards with agency staff at those sites to share with individuals looking to return to school. All materials featured the phone number for a hotline the Centers had set up to field inquiries and make initial referrals. Ultimately, the hoped-for increase in call volume did not occur.

The team also carried out outreach efforts by U.S. mail, to greater effect. Using an inexpensive approach, staff mailed friendly postcards informing students about the different locations to visit in their borough to discuss their options if they had considered returning to school or earning their high school equivalency diploma. The postcards generated traffic—indeed, many students entered the Referral Centers soon thereafter with crumpled-up post-cards in their fists.

A third means of outreach involved cold calls. The staff found this time consuming due to the volume of potential clients—one estimate showed that nearly fifteen thousand students could benefit from the Pathways to Graduation program. At times, cold calling proved discouraging, because a majority of the numbers on file answered "disconnected." Strong anecdotal validation for this approach did emerge, though, because so many parents and former students expressed that they were touched to receive a call and offer of help from the school system. For the future, NYC Referral Centers has concluded that cold calling constitutes a good approach for a small-scale, targeted effort.

NYC Referral Centers' most effective outreach technique did not involve students directly. Rather, the referral relationships that Centers staff formed with school counselors and city agencies helped create connections with the most students. In view of the current reality in NYC that not all students are on track to graduate, school counselors carry a heavy load trying to find options for all of their students to succeed. The team reached out to schools with higher proportions of students dropping out to make certain that faculty and staff at those schools knew about Referral Centers and the many alternative roads to a diploma in NYC.

Some at the schools expressed skepticism, many more, gratitude. From building these relationships, NYC Referral Centers has seen an increase in students enrolling in Pathways to Graduation programs directly from high schools, rather than dropping out of the school system first. And policy conditions in New York permit students to stay enrolled with the NYC DOE if they shift to prepare for the high school equivalency diploma.

In addition to schools, the team also developed fruitful relationships with other city agencies. The greatest synergy arose with three agencies in particular: Small Business Services, Human Resources Administration, and the Department of Probation. The first two agencies serve hundreds of thousands of New Yorkers looking for help finding employment and public benefits, respectively.

When education needs arise, frontline staff at these two agencies now know about Referral Centers as a resource for anyone who needs help sorting through options. Similarly, the Department of Probation provided opportunities to brief probation officers about how the Centers can help their clients finish their high school education.

GETTING REFERRAL CENTER VISITORS REENROLLED IN SCHOOL

In contrast to the Referral Centers' relatively new focus on proactive outreach, described just above, the Centers team in DOE has had a long-standing focus on increasing successful school and program placements after students visit the Centers. DOE works toward an ambitious goal: that every student with some level of motivation to continue school enrolls within the school year he or she visits a Center.

And yet, to provide a perspective on the referral-to-enrollment challenge, as of four years ago just 60 percent of the students referred to Pathways to Graduation actually enrolled. The team has regularly examined and unpacked data to understand the many reasons for nonenrollment, and has consistently drawn inferences from the data to guide creative solutions to support the transition back into school. This close underlying reliance upon data to guide practice constitutes the fundamental method by which DOE has nudged the enrollment number north of 71 percent.

The Referral Centers team has identified three crucial steps to monitor and improve outcomes—stated simply, these include:

1. Capture information on every student who visits.
2. Monitor outcomes on every student.
3. Disaggregate placement information to identify strong practices and areas of concern.

Capture Information on Every Student Who Visits a Center

In common with many if not most reengagement centers and programs, the Referral Centers establish a base upon which to track outcomes by collecting a range of information up front on everyone who visits, follow up on points of contact, and plan next steps. The Centers keep the initial form simple and quick; staff then enter the information into a database that in turn synchronizes with the broader Department of Education student information system. Of note, the most important information on the initial visitor form involves up-to-date contact information.

Monitor Outcomes of Every Student

With the information about a student entered into the database, Centers staff can track if the student makes it to the next step in their process, and if they eventually enroll in a school or program. Centers staff report that careful attention to each student—for instance, prompt followup after a missed appointment—can have a large impact on student follow through and progress. Specifically, NYC Referral Centers found that contacting a student within forty-eight hours of a missed appointment increases the likelihood of him or her enrolling by 35 percent.

Monitoring the outcomes of more than eight thousand students annually could easily prove overwhelming, so the Centers team has endeavored to use the data at its disposal in a few smart ways to aid the monitoring task. First, the team focuses on a specific numerical placement goal. In 2014-15, for example, the goal was to place 75 percent of all students referred, and the team reached the 71 percent level mentioned above.

Team leads post a monthly dashboard to show progress against the current year goal compared with the previous year. Getting to the finest-grained level, the team leads also provide weekly updates for each guidance counselor (the staff member who makes referrals) on which of their students have enrolled and which still have not. This consistent flow of information helps the front-line staff to gain recognition of the fruits of their labor, to save time looking up each student, and to identify exactly which students need followup and support.

Disaggregate Placement Information to Identify Strong Practices and Areas of Concern

At the administrative level, disaggregating the Centers' placement information based on who made the referral, as well as to what site the student received a referral, has helped gauge overall progress and suggests timely interventions and changes of course. A surprising variability in outcomes arises, and current practice involves monitoring and comparing these outcomes at least once each month. The range turned out to be quite significant when observing the monthly placement rates at each site—from 100 percent of students referred and subsequently enrolled to as low as 20 percent.

Visiting the sites with very high placement and mapping the communication between them and the Referral Center has helped to improve practices citywide. Additionally, intervening at sites as soon as the placement rate falls below the borough average has helped to clean up internal systems and strengthen accountability, so that more students successfully take this important step of enrolling back in a school or program.

REFLECTIONS, LESSONS LEARNED, NEXT STEPS

Initial discussions of placement rates among Referral Center staff produced the response that "a student is more than just a number." This statement appeared to reflect multiple levels of concern about items such as the balance between qualitative and quantitative evaluation of staff and programs, and comfort levels analyzing and understanding the implications of data.

Over time, the NYC Referral Centers staff team has come largely to agreement that data points can offer useful information to guide practice. Data occupy an appropriate place as one source of information, something that staff can now discuss in a more relaxed, less threatened context. Indeed, better using the data at the Centers' disposal has allowed staff to "work smarter, not harder," and focus more time collectively on helping students take an important step toward the life they want to live.

Going forward, the NYC Referral Centers team still has more work to do to reach youth across the city who could reorient and return to school, as the initial set of outreach efforts increased visitor flow into the Centers by about 6 percent. The team also needs to improve its approach to evaluating which outreach efforts work best, in which situations. Regardless, visualizing data on where these students live, in which of those neighborhoods more students and families need to know about Referral Centers, and from which schools more students drop out has already proven invaluable to help focus early efforts and better target the students who need help.

Another area for further improvement, certain to be guided by data, involves better completing the referral handoff and ensuring that students successfully enroll in school or a program. The NYC Referral Centers team has made considerable progress at the procedural level by recording information on each student's contact information and goals, then monitoring student progress and following up expeditiously. The challenge remains to push the enrollment rate up to and beyond the 75 percent level across the board, as already occurs at a number of receiving schools and programs, and then to sustain that progress over time.

Chapter Ten

Effectively Leveraging Institutional and Community Partnerships

Debra Duardo, Robert Sainz, Glen Biggs, and Judy Rye

In 2012, the Los Angeles Unified School District (LAUSD) and the City of Los Angeles, California, embarked on journey that resulted in one of the most significant partnerships between two enormous public systems. The partners developed a common vision to provide a systemic approach that would apply across the sprawling city for disconnected youth to reengage into school and work. The result: a high school dropout recovery *system*.

Over a similar time period, another approach to reengagement took shape in Nashville, Tennessee, one that brought together a different set of community partners. Nashville concentrated its efforts on organizing a range of service providers to provide supports and services, also in a systematic manner. This chapter, then, offers two complementary examples as to how cities of different sizes and characters can employ a concerted reengagement strategy and achieve promising levels of impact.

LOS ANGELES: FROM DATA TO COLLECTIVE RESPONSIBILITY AND ACTION

In Los Angeles, the path to creating a system included the following four elements: *capturing* the scope of the problem through data; *committing* to collective responsibility to find a solution; *acknowledging and embracing* collaboration as an ongoing process; and *leveraging* multiple local initiatives and resources. Three years on, the partnership has produced remarkable successes, including supporting more than two thousand students back onto sound educational pathways.

Capturing the Scope of the Problem through Broadly Shared Data

Well before development of a reengagement strategy began, Los Angeles sought to establish far more nuanced understandings about the city's population of opportunity youth—those ages sixteen to twenty-four, who were out of school and out of work—as well as the subset of that group who had left high school prior to completion. It sought this understanding in order to guide policy and practice. And given the city's size, strikingly large population numbers came into play.

The Los Angeles Unified School District holds the responsibility to educate almost six hundred thousand students each year, and has adopted the challenging goal of ensuring that every student is on track to graduate. One cohort-level examination of the graduating class of 2010 determined that more than ten thousand students who began high school had left school four years later. An earlier detailed study by labor economist Paul Harrington identified approximately one hundred thousand young people ages sixteen to twenty-four who are out of school and out of work.[1]

Harrington's emphasis on the economic and social implications of the crisis involving one out of five youth in the age group in Los Angeles stunned the highest levels of local policy influencers, and also forced and created discussion between formerly isolated advocacy groups. Harrington's specific findings noted that 93,013 young adult residents representing 19.8 percent of the city's total young adult population were out of school, jobless, and disconnected. By comparison, the national average at the time of the study stood at 14.3 percent and the California average at 15.9 percent.

In 2009, Professor Harrington and his associates updated their findings in two new reports: *Dropouts: Path to Poverty*[2] and *Update: One Out of Five*.[3] The key findings of the reports, straddling desired educational and labor market outcomes, included:

- *Lower employment rates for high school dropouts*: Among youth in the age group, high school dropouts were least likely to have worked at all during a given year. In the Los Angeles metro area, 70 percent of all high school dropouts had worked at some time during the prior year, compared to 78 percent of high school graduates, and almost 90 percent of college graduates. The work rate among female dropouts reached only 54 percent, compared with 85 percent among their male counterparts.
- *Lower lifetime earnings*: Calculations estimated the expected lifetime earnings in the Los Angeles metro area of a high school dropout at $697,000 compared to $1.2 million for a high school graduate. Projected earnings rose much higher with postsecondary certifications, totaling an estimated $2.43 million for those who earn a bachelor's degree and $3.5 million for those who earn a master's degree.

- *More years living in poverty*: Residents with a high school diploma spent an average of five years living in poverty, while those with a bachelor's degree spent an average of 2.2 years and those with a master's degree 1.5 years. The average number of lifetime years a female high school dropout spent living in poverty totaled 10.7 years—43 percent longer than the average length of time of the 7.5 years of their male counterparts.

This experience suggests the high importance for Los Angeles, and indeed, any city considering new strategies, to involve a broad group of stakeholders in identifying and analyzing data that capture the scope of the problem—and sharing that information broadly to prompt action. In Los Angeles, publicizing the city's high dropout rate shined a light on the significant number of students getting lost, and it also sparked a dialogue between the district and city.

In other words, the mutual access to information and sharing of data between the school district and the workforce development system provided a starting point to identify community needs and craft responsive strategies. The fact that this scan also identified high schools with the highest dropout rates, areas with high incidence of violence, high rates of uninsured, and highest rates of poverty, helped identify locations in which to target interventions.

Committing to Collective Responsibility to Find a Solution, and Following Through

Whereas excessive high school dropout rates constitute a national issue, responses and solutions must develop locally. Thus, one question arises as to who is responsible for providing the solutions. Various stakeholders in Los Angeles concluded—and followed through on—the observation that the responsibility lay not only with the school district.

Responsibility also attached to the city and county governments, the business community, policy leaders, elected officials, school administrators, community leaders, parents, and young people themselves. The vision involved all these groups coming together to provide solutions and strategies to keep young people in high school, increase college entrance rates, and identify career pathways for future employment.

Setting out a basis in policy helped make collective responsibility real. Two major civic proclamations, the Los Angeles Compact, led by the Los Angeles Regional Chamber of Commerce, and the Los Angeles Strategic Economic Development Plan, led by the Los Angeles County Economic Development Corporation, identified the development of a dropout recovery system as a major goal for education and business leaders, respectively.

The Los Angeles Workforce Investment Board and the Los Angeles Unified School District School Board have also identified dropout recovery as a major emphasis in their strategy outlines. The coalescing of these major institutions around a goal constituted an important step in building an interinstitutional system to recover the city's young people.

In addition to the focus on the young people themselves, some saw great importance in pursuing the dropout reduction goal as one contribution to the region's economic development efforts, and to increasing the quality of life for the future generations in Los Angeles. Dropping out of high school in today's economy has severe and unforgiving economic and social consequences for young people and the city as a whole. It was in the city government's interest to lessen the leakage in the educational pipeline, and simultaneously, implement strategies to return young people back to school.

Thus, in Los Angeles, the city department coordinating economic and workforce development efforts aligned goals to key policies and funding flows serving disconnected youth such as the Workforce Investment Act (succeeded recently by the Workforce Innovation and Opportunity Act). A related imperative involved identifying key decision makers in each system that would serve as champions in the development and implementation of this collaborative system.

With the above pieces in place, throughout the eighteen months prior to the official 2012 kickoff of what came to be known as the YouthSource System Partnership, both LAUSD and the city government engaged in the following strategies in an escalating spiral of productive activity. Steps included:

- Convening an advisory leadership team to guide the process and to provide strategic recommendations and implementation of these efforts.
- Supporting a community-wide volunteer high school dropout recovery initiative, "Student Recovery Day," as well as an ongoing volunteer mentor program. This got off the ground on September 24, 2010, and was implemented by LAUSD with the support of the mayor and city government departments. This effort alone returned more than 1,100 young people to school.
- Developing highly identifiable dropout recovery centers throughout the city of Los Angeles colocated with city- and community organization–supported programs funded under the Workforce Investment Act. These Reconnection Centers established multiple entry points for young people to return to school and work.
- Advocating for general and special grant funds for high school program counselors and dropout recovery staff specialists in LAUSD. Initially higher due to a successful advocacy push, the number of these positions

dwindled in more recent years due to decentralization and budget cutbacks.

- Identifying that colocating LAUSD Pupil Services and Attendance counselors in the Reconnection Centers would provide students with at least three critical services: 1) access to student records to understand, for instance, levels of credit accumulation; 2) an educational assessment and plan; and 3) links and referrals to onsite workforce programs. Placing trained LAUSD counselors in this role, even though working offsite from LAUSD schools, allowed for students to gain access to and release otherwise confidential educational records without violating FERPA regulations.

- Improving the coordination of secondary-community college bridging and pathway programs so as to provide reconnected students options to transition from high school diploma programs to community college or industry-credentialed certification programs. Experience gained through funding the Reconnections Academy through the American Reinvestment and Recovery Act provided one model now undergoing replication.

- Developing a citywide public campaign to reach out to the high school dropout population utilizing city and education leaders, including the mayor, LAUSD school board members, Los Angeles Community College Board Trustees, and representatives of the philanthropic community, among others.

Acknowledging and Embracing Collaboration as an Ongoing Process

Forming new partnerships at the system level creates excitement, and can also bring unique challenges given that individual systems usually operate independently. In this sense, collaboration becomes a process, not an event. For instance, even with leadership on board, recognizing and cultivating key stakeholders such as front-line staff members proved essential to ensure the implementation of the vision and overall goals of the new Los Angeles partnership.

The partnership encountered other challenges as well. These included the different schedules of school district staff and the nonprofit partners, initially differing goals of workforce and schools staff, and differences in target populations. The primary focus on disconnected youth created anxiety as to whether the city would achieve workforce performance outcomes. Logistical matters, such as which entity would provide office supplies to staff and who supervised LAUSD staff on remote sites, all had to be addressed.

As these issues arose, it proved important for all leaders to get involved in addressing and resolving them, together. Ignoring the issues presented too great a risk of front-line staff becoming frustrated and resentful. Collaborative decision making and checking to make sure everyone's input got heard constituted useful steps. Essentially, the need for ongoing communication appeared early, and remains as a pivotal part of the collaborative process.

The Los Angeles partnership also found shared learning a useful technique. A professional development needs assessment identified local experts in systems and opportunities for learning. Tapping into school district resources allowed the partnership system to gain access to specialized training topics such as Psychological First Aid, understanding special education, and how to create a Coordination Services team.

In addition, the school district staff gained new knowledge on the workforce system and key citywide initiatives such as the Summer Youth Employment Program. Staff for each system partner became "bilingual and biliterate," with the acronyms and alphabet soup of WIA (Workforce Investment Act), IEP (Individualized Education Plan), and SST (Student Success Team). Quarterly systemwide professional development meetings took place in order to support staff to provide students with the most up-to-date information, and to implement the most promising practices to serve students.

Leveraging Other Local Initiatives

Since initial implementation in 2012, several opportunities to expand the partnership and integrate initiatives to support some of the highest risk students in the community have presented themselves or responded to cultivation. The watch phrase of the partnership became "Don't Duplicate, Integrate." Thus, the LAUSD-city partnership has folded in efforts to support two additional groups of young people with heavy overlaps in the dropout ranks:

- Probation-involved youth who were transitioning back from Los Angeles County Department of Probation Camps and Juvenile Halls
- Foster youth, through state educational formula funding to develop an intensive case management program to provide counselors to increase graduation rates

In addition to these population-specific efforts, the partnership has integrated its activities with two major support systems, one run by city government, the other run by LAUSD. Namely, Reconnection Center efforts now provide and receive referrals from: 1) the city's FamilySource System, whose goals include increasing family income and increasing academic achievement for families with children ages five to seventeen; and 2) LAUSD's fourteen Wellness Centers, state-of-the-art facilities that provide free medical and mental health services to community members.

In summary, whereas many of Los Angeles's specific strategies may not represent new innovations, the full package represents the first coordinated, comprehensive, citywide strategy. Through this systemic approach, the YouthSource System Partnership has created an opportunity for nearly eight hundred young Angelenos to gain access to comprehensive education and workforce services.

The sustained collaboration has contributed directly to LAUSD's increased graduation rates, as well as a five-year reduction in the dropout rate. Perhaps most important, focusing on goals and coordinating and leveraging services has provided a changed environment and new hope for thousands of young people, so that they have a far better chance to achieve their personal and professional goals.

NASHVILLE: ALIGNING COMMUNITY RESOURCES AND ENLISTING REENGAGEMENT COACHES

Nashville's efforts began as early as 2007 in response to local concerns about the appalling 58 percent high school graduation rate, and developed through a structured process to *align resources* that the city has used to confront other educational challenges and opportunities. Key steps along the way have included convening stakeholders, conceptualizing and implementing a voluntary reengagement coach training approach, and undertaking a pilot from which to learn.

Bringing Stakeholders Together

In 2007, the local nonprofit organization Alignment Nashville formed the 16–24 Year Old Out of School, Out of Work Alignment Team (A-Team) to bring together stakeholders from across the community to use the Alignment process to examine data and develop solutions for aligning existing resources to reengage the sixteen-to-twenty-four population. This broad group of stakeholders included representatives from Metro Nashville Public Schools, Metro Nashville government, area community colleges, community-based organizations, businesses, universities, and adult education providers.

For background, Alignment Nashville exists "to align community organizations and resources so that their coordinated support of Nashville's youth has a positive impact on public school success, children's health, and the success of our community as a whole." Alignment Nashville has created a collective impact toolset—principles, structure, process, and technology—to achieve systemic change.

The 16–24 Out of School Out of Work A-Team began by asking questions: How many sixteen-to-twenty-four-year-olds live in Nashville? Who are they? How did we get here, as a community? How do we change this story, for the city and the individuals? How do we help the youth already disengaged? How do we prevent more youth from dropping out of high school? These were tough questions, but only by asking, facing, and owning the reality of the situation could this collective begin to formulate ideas that would become plans and lead to change.

Here's what the 16–24 A-Team learned: at the time of the 2010 U.S. census, approximately ten thousand sixteen-to-twenty-four-year-olds lived in Davidson County/Nashville, did not have a high school diploma, and were out of work. That figure has remained static since the 2000 census. Looking through an economic lens, the A-Team's concern only grew when it applied a finding that each disengaged sixteen-to-twenty-four-year-old represents a social burden cost of approximately $37,500. For Nashville, this multiplied to $375 million annually in lost wages and taxpayer burden.

With these large figures in mind, the A-Team undertook its first public initiative in 2011: a 16–24 Out of School, Out of Work Community Conference. This full-day conference brought together community partners that provided services—health, education, basic assistance, and more—to the older youth population. The goal of the conference: to build a community of practice focused on the dropout crisis, the youth and families affected, and prevention methods. The meeting of approximately 150 attendees represented the first time in the history of Nashville that stakeholders devoted to the sixteen-to-twenty-four population convened with a common purpose.

The synergy from the conference and the network of organizations and individuals began a community conversation that recognized that if the problem of dropouts and disengaged sixteen-to-twenty-four-year-olds was to be solved, it would require a collective impact strategy. The 16–24 A-Team considered reengagement models from other cities, but found no framework within which to apply those models in Nashville. In addition, the A-Team had no financial resources, only resourcefulness.

Coaching as a Viable Model to Meet the Needs of Opportunity Youth

To deepen its understanding of returning student needs, the A-Team surveyed opportunity youth in 2013 to learn more about the youth and the barriers they faced to returning to and completing high school. These survey results provided the A-Team with vital information about opportunity youth that became the motivation and foundation for a new strategic plan: Community-Based Re-Engagement Coaching.

Coaching is a widely used strategy for change, growth, and success for individuals and has expanded into business, industry, health professions, and education, yet it had never been applied to the problem of disengaged youth. The A-Team spent several months carefully exploring coaching content, practice, and outcomes and developed a three-pronged approach specific to the needs of opportunity youth, based on principles of coaching:

1. To write an Invitation to Participate™ (ITP™) inviting local organizations to participate in the first coaching pilot. The Invitation to Participate™ (ITP™) is Alignment Nashville's main community engagement tool. Alignment Nashville uses the ITP™ to explain the need a particular A-Team seeks to address, the population in question, and the request to the community for resources to support a particular tactic—in this case, coaching.
2. To create a coach-training curriculum based on the core competencies of the International Coaching Federation.
3. To create a resource guide that would specifically address the unmet needs of this population, as communicated in the survey.

Based on responses to the ITP™, the A-Team selected six coaches to participate in an initial pilot. The Re3 Community-Based Reengagement Coaching Initiative began in January 2015 and ended in June 2015. The coaches worked at six community organizations with varying missions and geographical locations. The organizations shared a common commitment to serve sixteen-to-twenty-four-year-olds and collectively provided a range of services such as supports for homeless or transitioning youth, and mental health.

Developing an agreed coach-training curriculum for Re3 constituted the second tactic. Members of the 16–24 A-Team came together to design and write the Re3 training program. This group included a professional curriculum and training designer, two leaders in adult education, a mental health professional, and one certified life/leadership coach. The curriculum of the Re3 Coaching Training used the core competencies of the International Coaching Federation for teaching across four intensive half-days of training with the coach trainees.

As the six-month pilot phase of the Re3 Community-Based Re-Engagement Coaching Initiative launched in January 2015, the A-Team paired each of the new Re3 coaches with an Re3 trainer. Trainers provided support through weekly check-ins by phone, email, or face to face, as well as through monthly group lunch-and-learns—coaches reported the latter provided some of the strongest supports. A message board system on the Alignmentnashville.org portal allowed coaches to communicate directly with each other and to see each other's conversations.

The inaugural pilot produced important lessons, which the A-Team and organizations involved will proceed to apply. For instance, some coaches found very limited opportunities to meet with potential returning students. In response, the A-Team will consider tiering and categorizing coach availability. Whereas some organizations typically work with a client for only one or two months—for example, emergency or crisis-based homelessness or mental health supports—negotiating a successful return to an education pathway requires long-term coaching, including sustained contact with the client.

The A-Team's Collective Impact report on the pilot identified several successes, particularly regarding the training and coaching process. The biggest win: 68 percent of the opportunity youth who signed a coaching contract remained actively connected with coaches at the end of the pilot. The effort to create a resource guide produced an initial list of thirty-two targeted services, which the A-Team will update continuously. With this initial proof of concept in hand, the second pilot of Re3 Community Based Re-Engagement Coaching will begin in February 2016, with a substantially larger complement of twelve new coaches joining the network.

As the only comprehensive reengagement strategy in Nashville, daunting tasks remain for Re3. For example, the 16–24 A-Team has set a target to reengage more than one thousand youth in the second pilot, and to support those young people to attain a secondary credential and move into college and career with a plan and focus. The potential payoff provides continuing motivation, if one harks back to the economic implications of the situation. If 50 percent of one thousand youth complete the process and obtain a job with sustaining wages, this initiative would save Nashville more than $18,750,000. That is a savings and investment figure that few could ignore.

NOTES

1. Neeta Fogg and Paul Harrington, *The Teen Disconnection in Los Angeles and Its Neighborhoods*, Center for Labor Market Studies, Northeastern University, November 2004.

2. Executive Summary at http://cdd.lacity.org/pdfs/Sep_09_Dropouts-execsummary.pdf; Alison Dickson, Neeta Fogg, Paul Harrington, and Ishwar Khatiwada, *The Lifetime Employment, Earnings and Poverty Consequences of Dropping Out of High School in the Los Angeles Metro Area*, Center for Labor Market Studies, Northeastern University, October 2009.

3. Incorporated into Paul Harrington, Neeta Fogg, and Alison Dickson, *The Fiscal Consequences of Dropping Out of High School in the Los Angeles Metro Area*, Center for Labor Market Studies, Northeastern University, June 2010.

Chapter Eleven

Principles and Approaches for Reengaging Two Overrepresented Indigenous Student Groups: American Indians and Latinos

Korinna Wolfe

A close examination of demographics in the field concerned with reengaging opportunity youth in education shows overrepresentation of several groups of students. Nationwide, American Indian, African American, and Latino students disproportionately disconnect from school, and could benefit from reengagement services and supports.

For example, a summary of the National Center on Education Statistics's 2014 description of Opportunity Youth by race—youth ages sixteen to twenty-four who were neither working nor in school and who had not attained high school completion—revealed that American Indians and Alaska Natives show the highest percentages of any group among opportunity youth at 19.7 percent, followed by 16.6 percent of Black youth and 14.3 percent of Hispanic youth. [1]

Within Portland Public Schools (PPS) in Portland, Oregon, the data fall out in similar proportions. Males of all races graduate at a rate lower than that of their female counterparts. Persistent predictable trends in outcomes by race remain strong; American Indian students consistently graduate at the lowest rate of all groups.

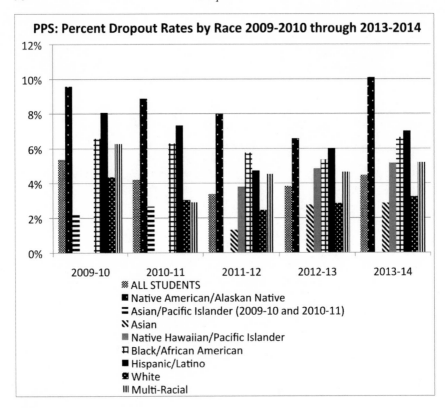

Figure 11.1.

As a cross-reference with the event dropout rate statistics in figure 11.1 and figure 11.2, at the conclusion of the 2013 to 2014 school year in PPS, 38 percent of American Indian male students graduated from high school with their four-year cohort, the lowest of all racial and gender pairs. Also in PPS in 2013 to 2014, 51 percent of Latino/Hispanic males and 55 percent of African American males graduated in four years with the peers with whom they began high school, significantly lower than the 62 percent of multiracial male students, 71 percent of White male students, and 76 percent of Asian male students of the same cohort.

Female students of all races fared better overall in Portland, yet troubling patterns have persisted along racial group lines, as illustrated by figure 11.2. For the same school year, 55 percent of American Indian female students graduated with their four-year cohort, along with 63 percent of Latina/Hispanic students, 65 percent of African American/Black female students, 70 percent of multiracial students, 80 percent of White students, and 88 percent of Asian female students.

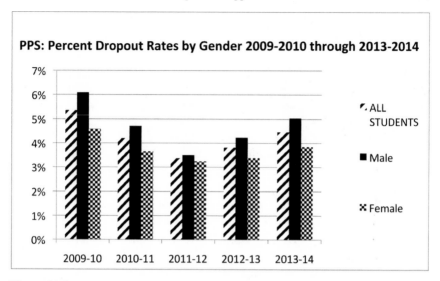

PPS: Percent Dropout Rates by Gender 2009-2010 through 2013-2014

Figure 11.2.

Adding to the four-year graduating cohort, those students who complete high school with a diploma or equivalent following their fifth, sixth, or seventh year of high school helps raise completion outcomes in PPS by more than 10 percent overall. However, predictability by racial group and overrepresentation of American Indian, African American, and Latino/Hispanic opportunity youth persist.[2] Additional populations represented among the ranks of opportunity youth include pregnant and parenting students of both genders as well as homeless students. Both of the latter groups may appear in multiple overrepresented categories.

Given the concerning gaps that Portland and many other cities need to close for particular groups in the opportunity youth population—including via special emphasis within reconnection services—this chapter describes principles and approaches for American Indian and Latino students drawn from experience and interviews in Portland, Oregon, and Newark, New Jersey, as well as from relevant research literature.

The limited scope of this chapter precludes listing principles and approaches for African American and pregnant, parenting, and homeless youth. As indigenous communities of North America, American Indian and Latino opportunity youth frequently experience similar issues of invisibility in education systems rooted in a monolingual, Western European framework. Subsequent attention to lessons learned from particular targeted efforts to reengage American Indian and Latino youth and others can provide additional insight and add to the contribution this chapter intends.

PRINCIPLES AND APPROACHES FOR REENGAGING
AMERICAN INDIAN YOUTH

As a result of the often tragic and culturally insensitive ways that formal education systems have treated Native American people since at least the 1870s, Native American students consistently report that they do not feel welcomed, supported, or acknowledged for their traditional or academic knowledge and talents. Too frequently, schools do not make specific attempts to engage Native families at their schools with activities that are culturally relevant, nor do the schools use curriculum that is inclusive and validating for Native American youth.

Moreover, parents and grandparents may have memories of physical abuse or emotional trauma associated with formal education settings such as boarding schools, as well as profound awareness of the derogatory context in which many curricula present American Indians. These conditions, among others, lead to a lack of consistent attendance and recurring academic success.

This background makes reengaging American Indian opportunity youth who have left or gotten pushed out of school extremely challenging. Further difficulty arises when students, as well as their parents and grandparents, may not develop aspirations for high school completion and postsecondary readiness if they perceive that it will come at the cost of individual shame for the student and the continued loss of family unity and tribal culture.

Nevertheless, it remains possible to identify several principles and approaches to improve the chances of success in efforts to reengage American Indian youth. These include: allowing time for listening and processing past educational injuries and disconnects, demonstrating genuine caring and cultural sensitivity, providing unrelenting care, and effectively utilizing the expertise and resources of federally funded Indian Education Program personnel. Adopting these approaches will pay off, particularly in the many cities such as Portland that are home to significant concentrations of American Indian opportunity youth, and perhaps in rural settings on or near Native lands as well.

Listen and Process Actively

When Portland Reconnection Center outreach coordinators meet with American Indian families, the initial conversation often features frustration, anger, and disgust with the educational system. The history of North American settlement has imposed an experience on American Indian people in which others make decisions that affect every aspect of Native lives, including access to education and employment. Outreach coordinators and others with experience working with the population report that they have found it vital to acknowledge the harm that has come to Native American students and their families through these decisions and the attendant disempowerment.

Listening and providing time to process historical memory, however recent, constitutes the best way to understand the experiences of Native families. As in other applications of "active listening" to gain a deeper understanding, this will involve mirroring back to families what the listener heard about prior experience. Processing can also take a forward-looking cast, so that taking opportunities to ask parents and relatives, "What are your hopes and dreams for your child?" and "What settings have worked well in the past?" will yield fruitful conversation.

Demonstrate Genuine Caring for Each Student and His/Her Tribal Culture

For many reasons, outreach and reengagement staff who end up working with tribal youth may not know how to pronounce tribal names, know the geographic base of a particular tribe, nor have an accurate understanding of the tribe's history. Given this situation, reengagement staff need to demonstrate genuine caring for each student and his/her tribal culture by making inquiries into each student's tribal affiliation, and by expressing a readiness and eagerness to learn about that affiliation. See the example in box 11.1.

Textbox 11.1 A Native American Reengagement Success Story

I had the experience of working with a Native young woman, Jaden*, who I'd met within the Native American community in Portland. I knew this young woman as a talented Lakota Fancy Dancer and had the pleasure of seeing her dance at our local Delta Park Pow-Wow in June. Jaden was in foster care and had been separated from her siblings, who were also in foster care. After being disconnected from school for a period of time and running from a foster home, Jaden was placed in a kinship foster home but was not attending school.

Learning this, I brought her some huckleberry jam and fry bread, two culturally specific foods common to the Oregon Native American community, from a Native gathering I attended the day before. Showing a genuine caring for Jaden mattered. It demonstrated that I saw her and cared about her tribal culture. As a result, she asked if I would speak to the kinship care provider and seek permission for her to attend weekly traditional Native dance classes at the local Native youth agency.

> The kinship parents and Indian child welfare worker allowed her to attend weekly Native dance classes with the agreement that she also attend tutoring at the same agency earlier the same evenings. Surrounding her with a caring Native community began her path back into regular school attendance and eventual high school graduation.
>
> * Name changed.

Articulating back what one has learned or knows about the tribe often proves meaningful for Indian youth. A knowledgeable colleague has observed Indian youth develop "truth meters" that are always on, and the staff person's level of genuine caring will undergo assessment throughout efforts to reconnect Native youth.[3]

Reengagement staff can also show caring and develop relevant knowledge in at least two additional ways. One involves finding the tribal people in the local community and making oneself and one's genuine interest in reengaging American Indian youth known. Gaining a better acquaintance with the local Native-specific agencies constitutes one tangible step toward finding tribal people and countering the all-too-frequent invisibility of Native Americans.

A second step involves learning about the local and state American Indian communities, so as to be able to answer questions such as: Where does the local Native American community gather? How many federally or state-recognized tribes live in the state or area? What types of "Trail of Tears" forced marches took place within the state? In Oregon, for example, few outside the Native community may know that the U.S. Army force-marched American Indians up the coastline from southern Oregon to northern Oregon; many people died along the way. This had the effect of moving peoples from their traditional lands to what now constitute the Grande Ronde and Siletz reservations.[4]

Provide Unrelenting Care and Stay Persistent

Often, reengagement staff will find that building a connection with American Indian youth and families requires great persistence, as well as an authentic attitude that keeps the student's well-being uppermost. PPS Indian Education director Karen Kitchen advises the following:

> Be unrelenting in your care of Indian youth. In this modern age we often rely on text and email when we really need to be face to face. The impersonal nature of text does not contain the possibility of true personal connection. Even when students come late, keep the focus on—you're here now. Let's focus on the fact that you are here and what we can do together here in this moment.

Staff can expect to hold multiple meetings in order to achieve progress. Notably, the topic of education may or may not provide the first connection made with a Native family. Bringing food or clothing to the family—finding some way to connect with the family—could result in making vitally important inroads.

Utilize School District Title VII/Indian Education Program Personnel

A fourth suggestion involves fully deploying resources for American Indian youth, which come to school districts through the federally funded Indian Education Program, known as Title VII. These programs may go underutilized in many districts. Whereas Title VII funding only supports small-scale staffing in most districts, those staff do have the specific responsibility and often the expertise to pursue successful school engagement and support for American Indian students and their families.

Portland, Oregon's experience may prove illustrative. In that city's main school district, the current Indian Education director has more than thirty years of experience. Because of her indigenous—Osage—lens and her longevity, she has built positive relationships with Native families that are multigenerational. She notes, "Showing the parents that you are on board with developing a plan and following through with the plan—showing not telling—is going to increase your success."

In best cases, culturally respectful and responsive staff members in a Title VII Indian Education office may often know the cousins, friends, and kin of American Indian students. When school district personnel have questions regarding where a family may have moved, if an American Indian student and his/her siblings and cousins got reengaged in schooling and if so, where, the Indian Education program often holds the information. Title VII programs can also assist district and partner staff to learn more about American Indian cultures.

PRINCIPLES AND APPROACHES FOR REENGAGING LATINO YOUTH

Recognizing and acting upon the vastly different needs of subgroups within the Latino community provides an overarching frame when considering principles and approaches for reengaging Latino youth. For some Latino families, documentation or citizenship rises to a profound level. The needs of Latino families whose ancestors have lived in U.S. territory for multiple generations—often preceding U.S. statehood—will likely differ.

Indeed, overcoming the misperception of a unified Latino bloc remains a principal task in order to avoid frequently incorrect assumptions regarding the level of Spanish and English fluency, family composition, economic stability, and standard of living. In a manner not wholly dissimilar to the "unwelcome other" position in which American Indian students and families too often find themselves, Latino students and families frequently feel unwelcome in school communities entrenched in monolingual culture.

Information sent home solely in English will not necessarily stimulate interest from Spanish-speaking families maintaining varied levels of English with sparse access to translation services. Schools frequently have diminutive translation budgets, limiting access to translation to occasional formal parent-student conferences—not enough to foster ongoing communication and positive relationships between parents and teachers.

Segregation may also exist as an important historical memory for Latino students and families. The case of *Mendez v. Westminster School District of Orange County* served as a precursor to the much better-known segregation suit *Brown v. Board of Education*. Yet many remain unaware of the segregation of Mexican and Mexican American children to separate "Mexican schools" in Orange County, California, and other locations until at least the 1940s. [5]

With this context in mind, key principles and approaches for reengaging Latino students center around several issues. These include "meeting families where they are" regarding documentation—for its own sake and to support forward pathways into postsecondary education, allowing families to lead on finding adequate sources of translation, exhibiting radical empathy, and connecting reengagement with strongly held values regarding work.

Attend to Documentation Issues If They Appear More Urgent Than Educational Steps

Undocumented Latino students have at times expressed fear that engagement in education systems may put their family at risk for deportation. Reconnection Center outreach workers experience Latino students communicating, "I can't go to college anyways so it doesn't matter if I graduate." Such statements mask the fear of placing themselves or their families at risk if they reenroll in school.

When Latino students share such concerns in Portland, the school district and Reconnection Center response involves refocusing attention on actual realities. For instance, pathways to attain documentation do exist, so Portland trains its outreach workers to a level of having a basic understanding of the Consideration of Deferred Action for Childhood Arrivals (DACA) process.

Making referrals to local agencies that can share information regarding the fees involved can also allay concerns—the three-to-six-month DACA process can turn out more affordable than families initially realize. Sharing the path forward by breaking down the DACA process step by step with families can build trust between the family and the outreach worker as well, and can decrease the families' anxiety regarding enrolling in school.

Let Families Lead with Translation

In cases in which an outreach worker establishes that a family needs translation services, finding out whether the family has a positive relationship with an individual translator constitutes an important step. A small group of translators typically operates in one city or neighborhood, and families bring specific prior experiences with them.

Exhibit "Radical" Empathy

Outreach worker Dennis Fournier proclaims that, for Latino families, showing deep empathy remains paramount. Fournier says, "You have to show 'radical empathy' to families. That you've been there and you have some human experience. [This also means] Showing up in jeans and a T-shirt versus a shirt and tie. I tell them some of my story, within reason of course, and let them know who and I am and where I come from. I have parents ask me, 'Do you know what it is to be poor and grow up in a ghetto?' And I tell them that I grew up in the South Bronx; Spanish Harlem. Then they feel like, 'Okay, I can talk to this guy.'"[6]

Connect Reengagement with the Collective Value People Place on Work

With Latino families—as with so many others—a strong work ethic is virtually universal. Families who state, "I don't want them to go to school versus work" regularly integrate new thinking when Reconnection Center outreach workers speak to the economic value of K–12 education. Explaining the combination of work and learning experiences and advancement opportunities that can ensue in a program such as YouthBuild, or in an alternative school with a Career Technical Education (CTE) strand, demonstrates the link between reengagement and providing for the family financially.

In summary, creating positive connections with American Indian and Latino students overrepresented in the current Opportunity Youth ranks allows reengagement programs nationwide to make a systematic, important contribution to equalizing educational opportunity for all. Strengths of indigenous communities need to be embedded throughout educational systems. Keeping key principles and approaches in mind for each of these distinct population groups constitutes a critical first step to using comprehensive, culturally responsive reengagement service delivery models. From this starting point, the Reengagement Network and its allies can help eliminate over-representation.

NOTES

1. nces.ed.gov/programs/digest/d10/tables/dt10_113.asp / table 501.30

2. Research and Evaluation Department, Portland Public Schools, 2015, http://www.pps.k12.or.us/departments/research-evaluation/5287.htm.

3. Interview with PPS Indian Education Director, Karen Kitchen, August 5, 2015, Portland, Oregon.

4. Confederated Tribes of Siletz Indians, "Forced Marches," http://www.ctsi.nsn.us/chinook-indian-tribe-siletz-heritage/our-history/part-i.

5. https://en.wikipedia.org/wiki/Mendez_v._Westminster.

6. Interview with Reconnection Services Outreach coordinator Dennis Fournier, August 15, 2015.

Chapter Twelve

Reengagement Center Practices: Lessons Learned on the Front Lines

Emmanuel Allen

Imagine walking into a building to have a discussion with strangers about what could be the most embarrassing, demeaning, and sensitive subject in your life. In this discussion, you may have to focus on information that does not necessarily highlight the most positive aspects of you as a person, or your decisions in the past. The expected result of this conversation is to reenter an institution in which you have not experienced much achievement, with no guarantees that you will be successful in the current attempt. This scenario represents the reality for many of the out-of-school youth coming to a reengagement center.

With these potential student sensitivities in mind, for the past nine years the city of Boston has focused on actively recovering students who have dropped out of school. The primary questions that guided this effort: Why did students leave school? And what happens as they try to return? The personal stories, reasons, data, and insights collected from reaching out to these students ultimately led early in these years to the creation of the Boston Public Schools Reengagement Center (REC), a full service center dedicated to recovering high school dropouts.

During this time period, staff of the REC—including me—have reached out to well over twelve thousand dropouts, conducted in-depth conversations with more than five thousand, and supported 2,335 to reenroll. Highlighting practical approaches, this chapter discusses the evolution of Boston's journey to recover dropouts, as well as lessons learned along the way.

EARLY LESSONS: LAYING GROUNDWORK FOR THE REENGAGEMENT CENTER

Helping expand the Boston Public Schools' Project Reconnect (described elsewhere in this volume) produced a number of useful lessons, which eventually informed the design and operations of the REC. These included:

Dropouts Want to Come Back to School, and They Also Want a Chance to Be Heard

Dropouts presented many different reasons for leaving school. Sometimes it was simple as not getting along with a teacher, or their family moved. At times the students described more complicated causes such as a death in the family or homelessness. The best strategy involved asking potential returning students to tell their story, and for the staff to listen and make no assumptions.

Giving a student a platform to tell his or her story from their perspective promotes honest communication, and also brings to light the real challenges that prevented them from completing school. One feature of Boston's reengagement team was that all the staff had either been dropouts or struggling students earlier in their lives, so they could get students to open up by telling their own stories.

Conversation Beats the U.S. Mail

Students who have dropped out usually need or want access to an alternative program to get back into school. Best case, these alternative programs offer the opportunity to complete high school at an accelerated pace. In Boston, several such choices exist—and the typical returning student is not sure where to apply, or which school or program would work best for them.

Whereas letters welcoming students back to school proved effective as invitations to return, sending out specific information about alternatives in an outreach letter produced more confusion then clarity. Many students and parents preferred having a conversation to sort through their options. See box 12.1 for an illustration.

Textbox 12.1
I remember my first intake vividly. It instantly changed the way I viewed my work. It began with a call in which I spoke to the grandmother of a student who was on the list of dropouts. I shared my

"former dropout who returned to school" story with her. After I finished, she asked where we were located. Within ten minutes, they arrived, and I was faced with the conversation that I had never had in person before.

During the calls I would tell my dropout story in under a minute, but I never went into the details. I made a decision to be completely transparent. I told the potential student exactly what I did not like about school, what I believed about it when I made the decision to drop out, and what I learned that made me return, try harder than ever before, and graduate at the age of twenty-one. He mirrored my honesty in the conversation and told me the reasons why he dropped out.

I could see a sense of relief on his face. He agreed to go back to school and give his education another try. His story ended up on the front page of the *Boston Globe*. Over the course of the summer we talked to a few more students in person, and these meetings were more powerful than our conversations over the phone.

Understanding Academic Standing Is Essential

Dropouts rarely looked at their transcripts and did not have a clear idea of the courses they needed to complete to fulfill graduation requirements. Some counted the years that they had spent in school, and assumed for instance that they were seniors based on the fact that they had gone to high school for four years. Upon reentering school, a student might find that she or he had freshman standing, which regularly prompted dropping out again.

Observing this pattern pointed to the role reengagement staff could play in interpreting credit accumulation for students. "Once we saw that a student had no credits, we could start preparing them mentally, rather than having them find out at their new school. We would emphasize that they could accelerate their progress to graduation in many programs. This made all the difference, and it increased the stick rate," says Wilson Santos, at the time the reengagement guidance counselor.

Placing Students into the Same District School from Which They Dropped Out Often Produces Unhelpful Conflicts

Reengagement staff met students who had undergone changes and matured during their time out of school. They had made an active decision to return to school based on these changes and were ready to try new behaviors and habits. When they walked into the doors of their old school, they were met by administrators or teachers who did not see this change and immediately assumed that the student was the same one who had dropped out before.

This placement of students into their original high school created conflicts that frequently led to students dropping out again. Again, observing the pattern led to the development of options to start over in a completely different school. Only in cases in which the student could restart based on good relationships and a high level of comfort did it make sense to return to the original school.

Dropouts Have the Academic Ability to Graduate

Massachusetts requires high school students to pass three "high-stakes" MCAS tests in order to graduate. Reengagement staff were surprised to learn that despite varying levels of credit accumulation, many students seeking reengagement had already passed two of the three MCAS tests. This demonstrated that for many, the issue was not lack of academic ability. Rather, it suggested the prevalence of nonacademic reasons for dropping out.

EARLY YEARS OF THE BOSTON PUBLIC SCHOOLS REENGAGEMENT CENTER

Based on the need and effectiveness of dropout recovery efforts, leaders determined that Project Reconnect should have its own location. One benefit of a freestanding location: students preferred more privacy, so that they would feel comfortable sharing personal information during conversations. It was a challenge to find a district building at first, so the Shelburne Community Center saved the day by offering space within its recreational facility. The community center also provided the use of its computer lab, along with a sizable multifunctional room, helpful for meeting with larger groups of students.

With a physical base of operations and additional investments, the reengagement team also expanded, growing from two to six staff members. Eventually the team also added its first female outreach specialist to provide an accessible role model for female students. This specialist also spoke Spanish, permitting better outreach to an additional group of previously unreached potential students.

BPS also supported the move by hiring a REC director, who would take responsibility for managing partnerships in the community and the school district. Having a BPS director on site also enabled access to vital, confidential information such as student transcripts. In addition, BPS added a guidance counselor to the REC staff, which provided the capacity to conduct academic assessments and support in the enrollment process.

Subsequently, BPS assigned a teacher to oversee classes on site. This addition permitted returning students to resume their education immediately, when motivated and ready, rather than remain on a waiting list. The teacher oversaw online learning, in turn aimed at helping students earn credits toward graduation rapidly and thus to sustain motivation.

As the team sought a permanent location, two considerations emerged. One was *provide your own entrance.* The REC's original location in the back room of the community center meant that students had to check in at the front desk to gain access. The process of checking in served as a deterrent to some young people. The team concluded that the REC needed a friendly front door of its own.

The second consideration was that *neighborhood and citywide accessibility matter.* It was important for the location to be accessible and well known in the community.

BUILDING TOWARD GREATER SUCCESS, FROM AN EFFECTIVE OPERATING MODEL

A subsequent move brought the team to a new location accessible by public transit and well known to families. The site housed a vocational school and several district and community service offices at a new location at Madison Park Educational Complex. This new location permitted the REC to continue scaling up its operations in an environment that the staff designed to be maximally youth friendly. A college library provided the model that the staff sought to create, with an atmosphere that was both productive and relaxed and respectful of students' status as young adults. With time, the REC also provided more specialized services and undertook special emphasis efforts.

One example of specialized services grew out of the recognition that connecting a dropout to an educational option was not always sufficient to lead to graduation. Sometimes students became separated from their schools and were not able to finalize all the steps needed to graduate and receive a diploma. REC staff intervened to help students complete the final credits needed online; partnerships with individual schools ensured that guidance counselors would check lists of requirements and clear students to participate in the school's graduation ceremony.

Increasing the "Stick Rate"

In addition to specialized services for individual students, the REC team set its sights on increasing the "stick rate" for returning students. Staff came to define this as the percentage of students that remained in school, or "persisted," for the full year in which they reenrolled. The REC's early stick rate was in the 30 percent range; in order to improve it, the team employed several strategies. These primarily played out in the schools in which students reenrolled, and met with increasing success up to the current yearly average rate of 70 percent or more students persisting.

The REC team has utilized several approaches over the years to support strong student engagement with the school in which she or he reenrolls. These included group workshops at schools that reenrolled large numbers of students. Team members also met with students individually, as often as once a week or once a month, depending on students' needs and the REC's agreement with the school.

Staff came to emphasize the "vital signs" of school engagement, in group and individual settings: school attendance, class attendance, and completing class work. Staff found that if they checked in and supported students to do well in all three areas, it was impossible to fail or lose ground. Supplementing the emphasis on the vital signs, REC staff also offer group workshops on topics such as the relevance of school, time management, relationship building, managing school culture, and learning to deal with others through the Myers-Briggs personality profile. Workshops build upon and offer opportunities to restate points that REC staff first made during initial intakes.

INSPIRING HOPE

Reengagement program staff is in the business of inspiring hope. The prospective student entering the reengagement center door, described in the first paragraph of this chapter, must hear words of encouragement when his or her life is not headed in a direction that accords with hopes and dreams. Experience to date serves as a reminder of how important it is for out-of-school youth to have the opportunity to look someone in the eyes and hear that it is not too late for them to achieve success in their lives, and that help exists to develop a concrete plan to reach success.

Nine years of working with people who are out of school has led to frequent witness of the effect that REC outreach and support can have on individual lives. At the aggregate level, a substantial segment of Boston's population—visible as one travels throughout the city—have received assistance from the REC to complete their education. Many have started families and embarked upon careers. Some are teachers and firemen, or work in airports, shopping malls, and city jobs. Virtually all now live lives that do not resemble their previous situations as dropouts. This reaffirms that in every city where students drop out, it is critical to have someone communicate the pathways to possibilities.

III

Emerging, Promising Practices in Reengagement

Chapter Thirteen

Using Workforce Connections to Reengage Disconnected Youth

Heather Ficht and Carla Gay

Some in the reengagement field, along with many others in the broader youth development sector, focus their inquiry and practice on how to support a key developmental task for young adults—to find one's way into the world of work and career. In Portland, Oregon, local youth workforce training and reengagement efforts increasingly operate on a convergence path, and the story of this convergence is worth exploring.

Notably, Portland has developed a variety of youth employment touches that appear to support reengagement efforts, and is also in the process of developing a collective impact approach to cross-sector investment and collaboration buttressed by a common accountability framework, which can provide an instructive model for other cities.

As background for this exploration, the nation's recent economic recession affected young people's employment prospects disproportionately and negatively. With youth employment on a ten-year downward trajectory already, the recession created a scenario in which young people with no prior work experience competed unsuccessfully with skilled dislocated adult workers.

By contrast, research by the Brookings Institution and others has highlighted the value of work experience for youth beyond earning a paycheck. Youth who work during their high school years experience higher high school graduation rates, receive higher lifelong earnings, and matriculate to postsecondary schools at higher rates than peers who don't. Early work experiences help prepare young people for life and future careers.

Indeed, many young people, particularly those who are disconnected from school, identify getting a job as a priority—yet they lack the skills and experience to obtain one. This provides valuable information as to what motivates young people, information that youth workers can leverage to promote educational reengagement.

PORTLAND'S CONTINUUM OF REENGAGEMENT AND YOUTH EMPLOYMENT STRATEGIES

Major institutional actors in reengagement and youth employment in Portland include the urban school district, Portland Public Schools (PPS); Worksystems, the local Workforce Development Board; and the city government and mayor's office and Portland Community College. A range of alternative schools and youth employment providers contract and collaborate with these institutions.

To provide a sense of scale: since 2009, Worksystems has put nearly four thousand low-income and/or reengaged young people to work. Portland Public Schools began intentionally reengaging out-of-school youth with the opening of its Reconnection Center in 2009, and has over time reconnected more than 1,200 youth with a variety of education and workforce training options. The two organizations estimate an average overlap of 50 percent between the groups of young people in question over the past three years.

In practice, Worksystems and PPS experience multiple points of intersection between workforce training and reengagement efforts. Reengaging disconnected or out-of-school youth in Portland occurs along one end of a continuum of services that both organizations provide. At other points on the continuum reside a variety of tiered prevention and intervention services designed to help in-school youth stay in school, graduate in four years, and persist in a postsecondary workforce training or education program.

Figure 13.1 depicts Portland's education and workforce training continuum, which flows generally from lighter- to heavier-touch services.

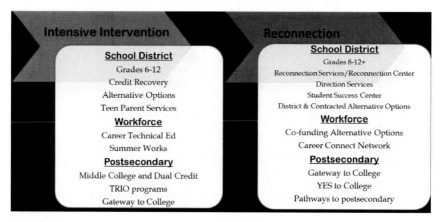

Figure 13.1.

As further context, the continuum of services depicted in figure 13.1 aligns with the PPS superintendent's three main goals: 1) all students reading at grade level by third grade (prevention); 2) eliminating the disproportionate discipline gap for students of color (intervention); and 3) accelerating the rate of high school completion for all students (prevention, intervention, reengagement).

In parallel and sometimes overlapping ways, Worksystems's lightest touch begins with career exploration through an online portal of business volunteers who are willing to come into the classroom or open their businesses to young people—Oregon Connections. The summer youth employment program, SummerWorks, provides paid jobs as a medium touch—see textbox 13.1.

> Textbox 13.1 About Portland's SummerWorks Program
>
> SummerWorks operates as a public-private partnership, in which federal resources, predominantly WIA/WIOA, support the infrastructure of the program. Youth work at job sites in local and regional government, the private sector, school districts, and others, most of which contribute toward the wages paid to youth. WorkSystems recruits low-income young people from ninety-plus different community-based organizations, alternative schools, and faith communities, as well as through mainstream high schools. Interns in SummerWorks may earn elective credit for participation if they complete a portfolio developed and vetted with all fifteen school districts in the region.

Worksystems's heavy touches come through support for career development services through a network of alternative school providers (many of which also contract with Portland Public Schools) for sixteen-to-twenty-four-year olds, with braided funding from a combination of WIOA, the Community Development Block Grant, and the City of Portland general funds.

HEIGHTENING WORKFORCE CONNECTIONS AND SUPPORTS TO AID REENGAGEMENT

The balance of this chapter zeroes in on Portland's reengagement approaches—what partners in the city have put in place to support those students who do not, for a variety of reasons, respond to the myriad of prevention and intervention services for in-school youth. Within the school district structure, PPS Reconnection Services focuses on reengaging students who have been out of school and need assistance in reconnecting to an appropriate educational setting to complete high school. Some of these students have been excluded from school due to a disciplinary incident; most have left school due to circumstances inside or outside of school.

With a mission to help every student find a path back to his/her future, Reconnection Services functions as the second-chance safety net. Building upon a long and rich history of partnership, Reconnection Services and Worksystems have sought more recently to leverage each other's strengths in education and workforce development in an intentional and strategic partnership.

The scale of need for reengagement supports is significant. In 2014 to 2015 alone, 2,098 students left a middle or high school for any number of reasons. Some of them enrolled elsewhere or reenrolled on their own, but others disappeared from the rolls. Reconnection Services contacted 1,047 of those who left, and reconnected 433. Of the 433, 89 percent remained enrolled or graduated by the end of the year.

One lesson learned from Portland's experience with education reengagement to date centers around the key role of the individual staff advocate, who works to build trust, remove barriers, and assist in reenrollment. A second lesson involves the importance of a strong data tracking and management system to document efforts and track outcomes. A third lesson involves the importance of establishing and sustaining a much more responsive and coordinated system, which prioritizes reengagement efforts and values the educational experiences of all young people.

Of note, the lessons described just above apply equally well to efforts to engage out-of-school youth in career development programming. Most youth don't know about their options to engage in workforce development programming. Many report that prior efforts to get help through public systems have not proved helpful and in fact resulted in reduced trust and confidence.

Early engagement in workforce development programming combines the information-gathering and partnering stages that take place during education reengagement, and typically also involves assessing youth's skills interests and career readiness to inform the development of a career plan. One contrast: youth generally see more immediate gratification from engaging in a "jobs program" because it represents the potential to earn money in the near term. An ongoing challenge for career development programming involves helping youth focus on longer-term career goals as well.

Beyond the frontline lessons, structural overlaps also exist between reengagement and workforce development efforts. Worksystems directs career development funding to some of the same alternative school providers that PPS supports. During the school year, educators use access to a Summer-Works slot as an incentive for young people to reengage in education. During the summer, educators may refer a young person to a SummerWorks job as a starting point prior to actual reengagement.

Reciprocally, staff members of Worksystems's contracted agencies regularly refer young people to PPS Reconnection Services. With the mandate under the new Workforce Innovation and Opportunity Act to spend 75 percent of youth funding to support out-of-school youth, the most common pathway for youth may begin with career development services and subsequently or simultaneously proceed into a secondary education option.

TOWARD COLLECTIVE IMPACT

As Worksystems and PPS continuously reevaluated the impact of their separate, sometimes interlinked, investment strategies, the managers for each agency's services to out-of-school youth identified steps toward better alignment of efforts to use resources more effectively and efficiently for better outcomes for more youth. These mutual goals served as the basis for a move toward a collective impact strategy. In addition to adopting common goals, early coordinating steps came at the structural and advisory levels.

For instance, Worksystems invited the PPS Reconnection director to serve on the local Youth Council, which guides the procurement of workforce contractors in the Career Connect Network. Similarly, PPS invited Worksystems's youth services lead to serve on a yearlong taskforce that looked at revising the accountability metrics for the contracted alternative schools.

As another step in forming the collective impact strategy, the task force provided indicators to accompany the common goals. Specifically, the taskforce created a new alternative accountability framework that names major metrics for success in programs supported by Worksystems *and* PPS. The metrics center on student academic skill growth, secondary credential attainment, and school connection in terms of attendance and persistence.

The strong, early steps toward a collective impact approach have highlighted what else needs to occur, beyond aligning contracts and metrics. The Portland partners want to continue driving toward a vision of a truly aligned system in which students who are qualified and coenrolled in both systems have access to the best of education and workforce training. Further leveraging local resources toward this vision creates an imperative to consider several more key actions.

One action involves fully coordinating what now operates as at least two parallel procurement processes, so that collectively, actors in the Portland metropolitan region issue a solicitation for the necessary elements of a career development *and* alternative education system. A coordinated solicitation would work best by utilizing data from a segmentation analysis of the struggling and out-of-school student population throughout Multnomah County, beyond the boundaries of PPS alone.

Access to broader data would permit soliciting the highest quality programming, intentionally designed to meet the demand for services for out-of-school youth in the communities in which those youth reside. The range of services would need to encompass efforts to meet the needs of younger students under seventeen years old who stand within reach of earning a high school diploma, as well as older students ages seventeen to twenty-four who require more workforce or postsecondary connections to complete a high school credential, persist in an education and training program, and perhaps get launched toward a postsecondary credential.

Another key action step involves ensuring that the tools for measuring accountability and the system for collecting data function in a streamlined fashion across contracted programs and between the two systems. This would permit the Portland partners to review and update their metrics system continuously for adjustments to growth, outcomes, and persistence while reducing dual data entry by staff. In addition, integrating this continuous improvement capability would increase local capacity to use the data to improve programming.

A third action step toward leveraging current outcomes, metrics, and data systems involves expanding the scope and capacity of the collective efforts. Ideally, this partnership needs to expand to include other systems such as the lead agencies for juvenile justice, human services, and the local community college district in order to support and ultimately reduce the number of out-of-school students.

Beyond these three key steps, and to aid the early success in formulating a collective impact approach, Portland is pursuing the development of statewide policy to incentivize all local areas in Oregon to invest in disconnected, out-of-school youth. In Multnomah County a promising collaborative effort continues to develop, focused on better services and supports for Opportunity Youth—those who are sixteen to twenty-four, out of work, and out of school without a high school credential. For the estimated three thousand young people who meet these criteria in the county, the broad collaborative, collective impact strategy, state policy development, and current braided workforce and education funding will prove essential to send a message that these youth matter and to back up that message with action.

Chapter Fourteen

From Reengagement, into College: Embracing Postsecondary Options for Out-of-School Youth

Nick Mathern, with Pam Blumenthal, Jahath Harriot, and Sue Stork

Over the past decade, reengagement of out-of-school youth to pursue high school diplomas and the equivalent has gained momentum and recognition as a critical strategy for building a comprehensive education system that legitimately strives to serve all students. Importantly, in a broader context, that momentum has been gathered alongside substantial changes to the economy and workforce requirements.

Going forward, high school completion alone is not a pathway to family-wage jobs. Instead, postsecondary education or training, whether in the form of an advanced degree or a technical certificate, constitutes the new standard. What is more, the overall education system has historically produced many fewer college graduates and highly skilled workers than the changing labor market requires.

Even as reengagement efforts have picked up steam, a separate, largely parallel education reform movement has taken shape. This movement draws upon educators and policymakers' recognition that the current bridges from high school to college are insufficient, and evidence has begun to be gathered that "starting college while in high school" raises college-going and college success rates. Indeed, numerous school districts and colleges have developed innovative partnerships that allow students to enroll in college courses and earn college credit while they are still in high school.

Once the domain of only the highest achieving and most motivated students, these opportunities have expanded dramatically during the past

decade. These partnerships take many forms: dual credit, concurrent enrollment, and early college have all established themselves as effective strategies
for high school students to practice and demonstrate college skills and begin
progress toward college completion. This has become a particularly effective
strategy for low-income and first-generation college students—a critical target group because they are otherwise underrepresented in higher education
and have historically achieved low postsecondary completion rates.

Whereas research and evaluation have demonstrated the power of providing early postsecondary opportunities for high school students, and policy
has responded with broad expansion of these opportunities, a continuing
divide exists. The chance to start accumulating college credits during high
school while practicing the success strategies needed on a college campus
largely remains reserved for otherwise successful high school students. To
date, too few intersections have appeared to create hand-offs or pathways
between the reengagement movement and the early college movement.

Now, however, a growing number of educators and communities across
the United States have begun to pull these two movements together, to create
a crucial overlap for the students who could benefit most from bridging
supports and the opportunity to complete a postsecondary certification. This
steadily growing group of innovators acts out of the recognition that attaining
a meaningful place in the workforce requires postsecondary education or
training. And these innovators understand that not helping all students to
achieve that outcome—especially the reengaged—would sell those students
short.

For instance, Gateway to College constitutes one of the most widespread
program models for supporting students into college-based reengagement.
Gateway to College started in Portland, Oregon, in 2000 through a partnership between Portland Community College and Portland Public Schools.
Since 2004, a network of Gateway programs has expanded to operate in
forty-one communities in twenty-one states. The Gateway to College model
includes the ability to complete high school credits and college credits simultaneously, in an environment of holistic student support for small learning
communities. In addition, other programs with similar strategies and structures have emerged independently across the country.

In each of the communities in which these programs operate, and whether
or not they come to Gateway or a similar program via a Reengagement
Center (most often, not), students seek to engage with meaningful and relevant activities. The out-of-school youth that Gateway recruits operate within
the same economic reality as their in-school peers. They recognize that postsecondary education has become a must for economic success.

Having left school does not mean that these students don't have the desire
or capacity for success in college. On the contrary, many of these students
have faced and overcome incredible personal challenges. A previous lack of

success does not stem from a lack of resolve. Rather, many such students have had to manage a broad range of adult-world obstacles in order just to get to the starting line for education.

This chapter provides "up close and personal" glimpses of the transformative power of postsecondary enrollment as a reengagement strategy, and makes the case for establishing the goal of reengagement well beyond the high school diploma. Structurally, the chapter features three voices, with three different yet overlapping perspectives on what it means to serve youth who have dropped out of high school by enrolling them in college: a student perspective; the perspective of a staff person who supports formerly out-of-school youth newly enrolled in college as a major partner in a local reengagement effort; and the perspective of the administrator of college-based reengagement programs.

By way of introduction to the contributors: Jahath Harriot is a young man who crafted a new identity and found crucial supports when he enrolled in the Gateway to College program at Massasoit Community College in Brockton, Massachusetts. Sue Stork directs the Northeast Iowa Community College (NICC) Dubuque Center, which hosts a high school completion portal called Re-Engage Dubuque, and whose college frequently enrolls formerly out-of-school students for HSED (High School Equivalency Diploma, which replaced the GED in Iowa) completion and career pathways courses.

Pam Blumenthal directs the Links Department at Portland Community College in Portland, Oregon. Her department spans programs including YES to College, a GED-plus program; the original Gateway to College program; Future Connect, a scholarship and support program that supports low-income, first-generation college students who have completed high school or a GED; and Project Degree, a program serving college students enrolled in Developmental Education.

The perspectives in this chapter come, respectively, from Massachusetts, Oregon, and Iowa, and suggest local conditions and nuances along the way. Separately and together, these stories illustrate the reality and the potential of pathways that allow formerly out-of-school youth to create new identities as successful college students.

JAHATH HARRIOT: NO LONGER FEELING LIKE AN ALIEN

At age eighteen I found myself lost, any trace of personal identity destroyed by years of turmoil. I was urged by people who cared about me to take my education seriously.

I remember feeling like an alien walking through the hallways and neatly trimmed gardens of Massasoit Community College. My first thought: I didn't belong here, I was a dropout south side kid just passing through because my parents were driving me crazy at home. It wouldn't be long before I would get kicked out. But that's not what happened. Instead, I found myself surrounded by people who cared about each other. We were strangers mostly: misfits and outcasts, young mothers, smart-mouthed corner kids, the goofys, the class clowns; and then there were the occasional shining stars—and everyone always wondered, "How in the world did these kids find themselves here?"

At the epicenter of this circus of unique, outrageous, and weird kids was the Gateway office. Inside that office is an amazing ensemble of women who somehow keep this place together. They are supported by a cast of professors who are every bit as colorful as the students. The freedom and opportunity of the community college experience, blended with high school fiascos and the craziness that sometimes followed students into class from their outside lives, all made Gateway to College life changing.

Education was all around us—in our mentors, our counselors, and our friends. I learned lessons in math, history, and science, gaining insights into a world of knowledge that I had been blind to for so long. I was learning to love learning again. Who would have thought it was possible?

My professors and counselors pushed me to improve myself and didn't accept my weak-ass excuses. I had to take charge of my own destiny, which intertwined with the fates of so many other memorable people along the way. The lessons I learned from other people were the most valuable. I learned to trust my instincts and to believe in my capability to grow mentally and morally.

By opening myself up and becoming friends with other Gateway students, I was able to see how others lived, realizing that I didn't have it as bad as I thought. I know what it's like to have no electricity when the bills went unpaid, but I had never had to sleep outside with a drug-addicted mother on a cold February night. I heard the gunshots outside my window every once in a while, but I had never held my brother as he bled out beneath the streetlights crying out for another day.

I, like many other Gateway to College students, have lived through a past filled with insecurity, failure, substance abuse, and violence. I can't say the scars we have are fully healed; maybe they will never be, but if it wasn't for the family we developed during our education at Massasoit, many more of us would be ruined. That is why it is absolutely necessary that we keep the spark of education alive so that it may engulf the hearts and minds of future generations.

It's easy to point fingers and judge students who have failed in a traditional educational setting, but we need to remember that there is a cause to every effect. Why are so many of our young finding it difficult to succeed? Pinpoint the causes, whether it be poverty, lack of motivation, or negative social conditioning . . . then confront them. That is what Gateway to College is doing, both in my local streets and cities and towns across the country.

Through Gateway, I have had opportunities to travel to conferences, and I met Gateway students and educators from across the country. I was in awe when these students told me their stories, of how they had overcome struggles that are very similar to the ones we are facing in Brockton. Somehow Gateway to College had been successful in changing the lives of youth in completely different states. This is all the evidence we need in recharging our belief that the combined efforts to help and educate "at risk" youth are well worth the struggle.

Reengagement into an educational and supportive environment brought so much value into my life and the lives of many students I know. Education is providing *all* those who seek growth and knowledge with a platform to reach their goals, even the hard-headed ones like me who had to bump into the platform a couple times before thinking to climb it.

SUE STORK: THE SUCCESS MODEL

The Re-Engage Dubuque program started in 2011 with a single coach, funded with state dropout dollars, using a cell phone, a laptop, and his personal car. Rather than waiting for students to find him at a reengagement center, the reengagement coach traveled throughout the community and used a variety of means to find and reengage out-of-school youth. Over time, the program has grown to employ two reengagement coaches, whose positions the Dubuque school district and Northeast Iowa Community College (NICC) jointly fund.

As Tom, the first coach, once said, "I do just about anything—short of being issued a no-contact order—to find and talk to students." Re-Engage Dubuque coaches meet youth in parks, at the YMCA, in coffee shops, walking down the street in groups, and by knocking on doors, making phone calls, and using social media. Word of mouth is the best recruitment tool. A reengaged student can post something on Facebook about going back to school, and suddenly, a cousin, a friend, or a sibling surfaces, asking about the program.

Reengaged students who decide to pursue a high school equivalency diploma (HSED) enter the HSED program at NICC with the support of a reengagement coach. At the centrally located NICC downtown center, these students study in a diverse environment that simultaneously serves college-degree, short-term certificate, HSED, and prospective students, all in the same space.

The philosophy at the college, referred to as the Success Model, is that *all students can learn if given the right opportunities*. Teachers, staff, and coaches take on the role of helping students determine the type of education or training to pursue, given their goals, abilities, and personal circumstances. Then, the NICC-based team supports students as they work to overcome barriers to their success.

Reflecting on how to make the reengagement process "stick," Temwa, another coach, has commented, "For me, it's about finding the emotional hook that will motivate the student." For example, one student, Darius, showed inconsistency about working on his HSED until his girlfriend got pregnant. He wanted to be a better father than his own dad had been, so he buckled down and got to work.

Once Darius had already completed the HSED program, he became eligible for a scholarship that paid for a short-term welding certificate program at the college, which he pursued with the support of a success coach. By the time Darius's baby came along, he had obtained employment in an entry-level welding job and enrolled in NICC's two-year mechatronics degree program with financial support from his employer.

Notably, NICC positions reengaged students as "automatically on track to a postsecondary credential" by connecting them intentionally with a success coach, who in turn helps each student see a range of opportunities they might not have previously known about, or considered. Together the student and coach create a career pathway map that demonstrates an outcome for every potential step the student may pursue. Meanwhile, the student's self-esteem increases with each achievement in the HSED program. Sooner or later, the students realize that other students who were once in their circumstances have completed the HSED and have now enrolled in a college program.

In another good example of effective reengagement coaching, coach Mike found a way to connect immediately when prospective student Josh arrived for their first meeting carrying a skateboard. Mike asked, "You longboarded down here?" and mentioned that his nephew was a long board skater. He used Josh's passion about skateboarding to steer the conversation toward Josh's goals. The two still share long board stories as Josh pursues his HSED, and Josh hopes to run his own skate shop someday.

Mike and an NICC success coach have helped Josh create a career pathway map that shows tangible steps toward that goal. With his HSED, Josh can get a job at a skate shop for some experience and work that job part-time while earning an associate's degree at NICC. With an associate's degree, Josh will qualify to apply for a management position at the skate shop, which he can do while completing his bachelor's in business or finance at a local four-year institution. When Josh is ready, he can take advantage of the Small Business Development Center services that are offered in partnership with NICC.

At NICC, so far, neither students nor faculty find a formal bridge or transition program necessary in order to get reengaged students into postsecondary education or training. Nor has Dubuque established a physical reengagement center. If one small city in Iowa provides an example—which may also apply to rural school districts—the "virtual" reengagement model works out, fiscally and logistically.

PAM BLUMENTHAL: A SYSTEMIC ORIENTATION TOWARD COLLEGE SUCCESS

The Portland Community College (PCC) Links Department began developing student support and success programs for opportunity youth more than twenty years ago. The past ten years have witnessed several visionary leaders coming forward to help with program design, improvement, and expansion because they embraced the need to create innovative strategies to reengage opportunity youth directly into college programs.

Along these lines, PCC's Gateway to College and YES to College programs have attained recognition as local and national promising-practice models for student support. Both programs involve close working partnerships between the college and local school districts to help young people learn the skills necessary to obtain their high school diploma or GED in a college setting while planning for their future career.

Keys to the success of these programs include: the individualized personal support provided by college success coaches; the shared vision as to what constitutes success that PCC has developed with its school district partners; and collaborative relationships fostered over many years to support programs toward success in ways that each system could not achieve on its own.

Some youth entering PCC Links programs lack the academic skills and habits to attain success in college. In response, PCC's college success coaches provide structured support that helps students navigate college pathways. The coaches teach college success and career development courses, and also provide advising and mentoring. They practice intrusive advising and meet with students on a regular basis, *and* also connect by text, email, and social media.

Coaches have caseloads of fifty to seventy-five students and get to know each student's personal story. Many of these students enter Links programs with low self-esteem and the feeling that college is not for them. One of the principal roles for the coach: to express and personify an unqualified belief in the student, until that student becomes able to believe in themselves.

Sometimes the question arises, "How can students who have not succeeded in high school achieve success in the rigorous, adult environment of college?" The experience of building the components of the Gateway to College program model provides part of the answer—that students can overcome many of the barriers that have prevented high school success, *with the right environment and support.*

Students with strong academic skills who must deal with significant personal challenges may find themselves leaving high school early, or never entering in the first place. Leah, for instance, came to Gateway after obtaining her GED. She had attended home school, or no school, for most of her life. She had many academic gaps, yet expressed an eagerness to learn and a strong commitment to her dream—of becoming a teacher!

Marcus, by contrast, had tried several alternative programs before he enrolled in Gateway. He had lived on his own since age sixteen, and at eighteen, he still lacked six credits needed to earn a high school diploma. He had a criminal record due to some drug offenses, and sought a place where he could start fresh and realize his dream of graduating college.

Leah and Marcus both struggled at times, yet with the structure and support provided by Gateway staff, they persisted. Leah has now earned a master's degree and works as a special education teacher. Marcus completed his diploma in one year and remains enrolled in college. The varying individual perspectives and numerous case studies that this chapter presents amply demonstrate the importance of not reserving college-based programs for high-achieving students.

In fact, the programs and models described here transform struggling students into high achievers. Thousands of students across the country who enroll, progress, and often succeed in these reengage-into-college programs have "voted with their feet" in favor of a combination of a relevant postsecondary opportunity and a supportive relationship with a caring adult.

Indeed, Opportunity Youth find the college elements of these programs and models attractive, and the personalized student supports make the difference in ensuring their academic success. Developing programs with students at the center, and hiring staff who are passionate about finding ways to help students succeed, remain key ingredients.

And although relatively uncomplicated ideas inform the initial development of these programs, it takes community partnerships and collaborative funding strategies to sustain successful programs. The experiences and testimony of Jahath, Sue, and Pam can readily inspire other communities to build similar paths for more out-of-school youth as well.

Chapter Fifteen

Early Lessons for the Field

Examples from High-School-Equivalency-Plus Programs in Massachusetts

Jennifer Poulos, Chad d'Entremont, and Nina Culbertson

A high school diploma or equivalent credential has become necessary for full participation in today's global economy, yet attaining such a credential hardly guarantees success. By 2014, estimates suggest 64 percent of all jobs will require more than a high school degree.[1] Policymakers and youth service providers, sensitive to these trends, have increasingly shifted their focus from secondary school completion to college and career readiness and persistence. The goal: to ensure all students can participate in postsecondary education and training that leads to financially sustaining careers.

For the growing field of high school equivalency (HSE)–plus providers, heightened expectations for students now appear necessary to fulfilling providers' missions, and a daunting challenge. HSE-plus providers tend to serve youth with significant and varied academic and nonacademic needs, including "opportunity youth" in need of education reengagement that have dropped out of school and remain unemployed and often disconnected from critical social services. Expanding programming beyond academic remediation, test preparation, and student supports requires building new capacities, despite limited resources. Many providers may struggle to offer services that promote success at the postsecondary level.

Recognizing this challenge, we conducted research on promising approaches in Massachusetts to developing robust HSE-plus programs that equip youth to participate in postsecondary education and the workforce. Findings shared in this chapter draw upon a larger body of work produced by the Rennie Center for Education Research & Policy, and build on previous examinations of the HSE-plus field, such as the Jobs for the Future "Back on Track to College" framework and MDRC's documentation of GED-plus programs.

Previous research on HSE preparation has shown great variance in student outcomes. Successful programs report HSE attainment rates from roughly 40 to 60 percent, yet those with the highest completion rates often attract the least disconnected youth. Ultimately, a paucity of information on effective practice and appropriate outcomes led us to ask: What practices among HSE-plus providers lead to better outcomes for reengaged youth? And what resources will programs need to develop and pursue the more ambitious goal of supporting successful postsecondary and career transitions?

In considering Massachusetts's capacity to serve reengaged youth, we took a close look at HSE-plus programs in three communities, examining to what extent local programming reflects promising practices and identifying capacity-building needs. To do so, the Rennie Center first developed a framework of effective HSE-plus practice elements, focusing on four critical program elements identified by literature:

- For academic development, flexibility, clarity, and individualization matter.
- Wraparound supports are essential to student success, because stability and safety precede learning.
- A career preparation and work emphasis provides a meaningful context.
- Postsecondary transition supports extend well beyond applications and access alone.

Using data on local supply (e.g., availability of adult basic education services) and demand (e.g., dropout rates, HSE test rates among high school students, and college enrollment rates), we chose communities with diverse population characteristics—including Greenfield, New Bedford, and Boston's Roxbury neighborhood—for closer examination of existing program offerings.

Rural Greenfield, Massachusetts, hosts a tight network of agencies working together to serve its sizeable population of Opportunity Youth. Offerings include a mix of highly structured HSE preparation courses and career-readiness workshops as well as programming that connects youth to the range of services they need. New Bedford, a small city with one of the highest annual dropout rates in the state, offers fewer education programs for opportunity youth. The city features a large number of community services aimed at alleviating poverty, yet existing outreach and retention efforts do not reach the large population of pregnant and parenting teens.

Boston's Roxbury neighborhood has among the highest poverty rates in the city and some of the lowest rates of employment and educational attainment. The Roxbury community benefits from several HSE providers, offering the advantage of proximity and safety with programming located in the neighborhood.

For the three focus communities and likely many others, this research points to a need to develop stronger bridges to postsecondary training and education; stable and sustainable funding arrangements; partnerships to meet multiple needs of youth; and caring adult staff who connect with youth throughout the reengagement process. Notably in terms of nationwide applicability, all three focus communities were small in scale and operating under resource constraints.

HSE-PLUS PROGRAMS

Throughout this document, the Rennie Center uses the term *HSE-plus* to denote a program or service that provides academic services in preparation of a high school equivalency exam, as well as other services that support youth to achieve other goals—such as wraparound connections, postsecondary enrollment, or career training. In the past, many might have referred to such programs and services as *GED-plus*, in reference to one well-known high school equivalency exam.

For the major phase of local inquiry, we selected programs in target communities if they exhibited elements of HSE preparation (academic development) with two or three additional supports (wraparound, career, or postsecondary transition). Rennie Center staff then interviewed representatives from each program to gain program leader and practitioner perspectives. Table 15.1 describes programs, by community.

Table 15.1.

Greenfield Program Profiles

Pathways to Massachusetts Comprehensive Assessment System (MCAS) Success	Serving about one hundred youth at a time, this program focuses on those who have not yet completed a high school diploma or equivalency and have not passed one or more portions of the MCAS exam. The program offers MCAS tutoring and HSE preparation.
WIA Youth Programs	Serving youth who meet one or more federal Workforce Investment Act (WIA) eligibility criteria (e.g., low income, receiving public assistance, homeless or in foster care, parenting), this program assists seventy to eighty youth per year. The array of offerings includes HSE preparation, job readiness and skills training, and job application support.

Roxbury Program Profiles

GED Plus	Aiming to empower up to fifty youths a year, this program provides the academic skills needed to achieve HSE, as well as the social competencies to advocate for themselves in the face of discrimination or other challenges.
X-Cel Education	Providing customized academic instruction and extensive college preparation and induction support to help low-income adults over age eighteen achieve high school completion and enter college-level study, this program serves around 250 youth per year.
YouthBuild Boston	Headquartered in Roxbury, this program provides job training, HSE preparation, leadership and community service opportunities, and life skills curricula to thirty to sixty youth per year.

New Bedford Program Profiles

ACHIEVE! Youth Opportunity Program	Located at the New Bedford site of Training Resources of America, this program provides a comprehensive array of services for fifteen to thirty out-of-school youth.
YouthBuild New Bedford	Providing thirty youth with supports toward earning high school equivalency and entrance to postsecondary pursuits as well as skills in carpentry and green building.

Most of the youth in participating programs range in age from nineteen to twenty-two, come from low-income families, are unemployed, and left high school without a diploma. The majority in the New Bedford and Roxbury areas are students of color. Greenfield's students are also disproportionately students of color relative to the town's population. Other characteristics of youth engaged in participating programs include:

- Highly mobile, with periods of homelessness
- Court involved
- Learning disabilities (many received special education services while in public school)
- Emotional, social, and behavioral challenges
- Medical or mental illness
- Limited/no family support, adult support, and social support

The programs attempt to serve nearly all youth who come through their doors. They did not report turning many students away for academic reasons. For recruiting, most programs relied on word-of-mouth recommendations among participants and referrals by partner agencies.

Program Content and Emphasis

Examining organizations across the three focus communities helped to confirm the importance of programs providing students with all four critical program elements identified above—academic instruction, wraparound supports, career orientation, and postsecondary supports—to foster successful HSE outcomes. A brief summary of more detailed program characteristics in the Massachusetts programs, alongside lists of typical characteristics drawn from the available literature, follows.

Academic Development: Multiple Options. To meet the academic needs of their students, HSE-plus programs often offer both part-time and full-time academic programs, focusing on curriculum and instructional practices that support mastery of HSE standards. Many programs also offer courses at pre-HSE levels, including basic literacy or English as a second language.[2] Instruction is highly individualized, and structure and dosage varies, allowing students to move at their own pace and work toward clear learning objectives.[3]

Upon student entry, most programs under study use the Test of Adult Basic Education (TABE) and other internal measures to group students of similar academic ability levels into cohorts and refer them to external organizations' services as needed. Programs typically offer regularly scheduled courses in one or more of the following academic areas:

- *HSE preparation*: Most programs have developed their own HSE-prep curricula, incorporating academic skills beyond the actual test and meeting curriculum guidelines required by funders. Programs offer small classes, led by a teacher who differentiates instruction to individual needs. As an example, one program uses the Kahn Academy online learning program to supplement instruction, although technology challenges limit its use.
- *Supplemental and informal academic services*: Programs provide additional academic services based on need, including one-on-one tutoring, subject- or skill-specific courses, and independent test prep using HSE materials. Programs offering these services tend to offer less-comprehensive HSE preparation courses.
- *HSE practice assessments*: Several programs ask students to take multiple practice tests until they are familiar with the content and structure of the test. They only refer them to an HSE test provider when students have proven themselves ready.

Wraparound Supports: All Hands on Deck. Effectively serving a youth population with multiple challenges requires more than academic support, including an array of services addressing basic needs and social and emotional well-being. Programs must put into place appropriate stabilizing supports that address the wide menu of challenges students face as a precondition to engagement in learning.[4] Successful HSE-plus programs create a safe environment for learning and provide tailored supports.

Participating programs work with partner organizations and use internal resources to deliver wraparound supports themselves, including:

- *Case management*: Some organizations employ trained social workers; in others, staff take on case management responsibilities. Case managers do everything from helping youth fulfill basic needs to providing one-on-one counseling and managing referrals to external agencies.
- *Advising and mentoring*: Staff typically serve as informal advisors and mentors to the youth they serve, building trusting relationships through which they can model behaviors and strategies youth need to be successful in life.
- *Life skills development*: Some programs teach life skills as a formal course throughout the week, focusing on such topics as financial literacy, self-advocacy, and nutrition. Across all programs, staff share a goal of developing internal resources, such as resilience and agency, so youth are able to manage future challenges and pursue their goals.

Career Preparation: A Range of Intensity. Many youth enter HSE-plus programs with the goal of improving their employment prospects. Effective programs vary in the extent of their career emphasis: some focus on job exposure, while others emphasize vocational training. Some leading programs use career-related topics to ground the academic curriculum.[5] Curricula that "contextualize" academic skills within work-related scenarios show improved performance in subsequent coursework and program retention and completion, as well as an impact on future earnings.[6]

Participating programs vary in how they approach career preparation. Most have found that career content—introducing career options, job-readiness training, and job placement—helps motivate students,[7] so even programs that do not have a specific career focus often integrate this career-relevant content into their programming. The range of supports include:

- *Contextualized curriculum*: Most programs shape academic courses to reflect students' career goals, teaching core content in the context of work-related topics.
- *Career advising*: Many programs offer job-readiness workshops and individual coaching, providing resume and interview support, work skills assessments, overview of trends in the local labor market, and opportunities to observe and practice professional behaviors and norms. Several refer students to partner organizations to provide these services.

- *Job connections and apprenticeships*: Some programs play a role in connecting youth with local employers and job opportunities. If job-training services aren't offered in-house, they refer youth to partner organizations where they can access more comprehensive career support.

Postsecondary Transition: A Critical Area of Need. Effective HSE-plus providers do more than help students get into postsecondary programs. They understand that many students will need ongoing support to complete a degree or certificate. These programs assist in application, enrollment, and persistence with a curriculum that incorporates college-ready skills, instruction to navigate postsecondary systems, application processes, and financial aid, as well as ongoing support after students have matriculated.[8] Program models such as these show increased rates of HSE completion, college enrollment, and college persistence when students have these additional supports.[9]

Only one participating program—X-Cel Education in the Roxbury section of Boston—emphasized postsecondary support as a core part of its programming; most programs offered only a few pieces of the elements below. The postsecondary transition services these programs provide include:

- *Campus visits and information sessions*: Several programs plan visits to local campuses to observe classes, meet staff, and demystify the college experience. Programs also host visits from staff of postsecondary programs, who introduce participants to the variety of degree and certification programs.
- *Enrollment support*: Several programs offer college admissions workshops and one-on-one support with applications, financial aid forms, and other admission requirements. Some programs administer the Accuplacer test, used by public institutions of higher education to assess the skills of incoming students to help students see where they stand on skills required for credit-bearing coursework.
- *College skills development*: Some programs offer college preparation courses and workshops that teach students college-ready skills, such as critical thinking and oral presentation. They also teach skills related to organization and managing a college workload.

THE PATH FORWARD: THEMES FROM PROGRAM INTERVIEWS

The Rennie Center's scan of HSE-plus programs in three Massachusetts communities revealed substantial overlap with what previous studies have reported about best practices in educating opportunity youth. Interviews also exposed several additional themes that may not be unique to these communities and will be important to consider for those seeking to create new pathways and expand existing programs to meet the needs of opportunity youth.

Postsecondary Bridging Strategies Have Yet to Take Hold Fully. A small subset of programs offers postsecondary preparation utilizing academic curriculum and supplementary offerings. Research suggests that continuous support through college is critical to postsecondary outcomes; programs participating in this study did not systematically provide such offerings. Of these programs, only one had an explicit postsecondary transition goal and provided the comprehensive support youth need to prepare, enroll, and persist to completion.

Many Young People Face Challenges to Sustaining Engagement with Programs. Youth play a role in setting their own goals in each of the participating programs, and staff work with youth to set goals during the enrollment stage. Because students begin in different places and have different aspirations, the length of their commitment varies. Staff generally encourage students to attend the program as often as possible to accelerate their progress, but not all youth who enroll prove able to sustain the commitment necessary to reach their goals.

Wraparound Support Makes a Difference; Partners Provide Critical Linkages. Program staff note that wraparound supports often constitute the most influential factors contributing to program success. Youth who get connected to other services are most likely to achieve educational goals: they are likely to have their basic needs met and obtain the assistance they need to troubleshoot new challenges.

However, program staff emphasized that they do not try to meet every student need in-house, instead aiming to utilize the resources in their local communities to provide the array of wraparound support youth need. External partners provide a range of supports, including financial assistance with basic and academic needs, connections to critical services, additional academic support, career supports, and postsecondary supports.

Variable Financial Support Limits Capacity for HSE-Plus Programs. Although the three programs do serve some school-aged youth and seek the same goals as public high schools, they subsist on funds gathered from a wide variety of sources. This study revealed funding so inconsistent that programs could shutter unexpectedly, leaving a portion of the opportunity youth in that community not served. For example, Greenfield's Pathways to MCAS program did not receive requisite funding and shut down operations in August 2014 after fifteen years. Struggles such as this underscore that HSE-plus programs fall squarely outside of the public education system, leaving programs with the continual challenge of funding programmatic offerings.

Staff Who Build Strong Connections with Youth Constitute a Critical Element. Regardless of role or responsibilities, program leaders expressed the importance of having staff skilled in forming bonds with students and promoting positive youth development. Programs typically employ small numbers of staff (one to four individuals), and all employees play an important mentoring role. A few programs employ young adults with similar life experiences to the youth served; these adults serve as valuable resources to engage youth.

The path forward for engaging opportunity youth in HSE-plus programs looks challenging. Providers already struggle to meet the significant and varied academic, social/emotional, and overall well-being needs of youth who left high school without a diploma. Current Massachusetts programs offer promising community-based approaches that can guide local and national efforts to create strong bridges to and through postsecondary completion to support these youth. Documenting the work of these communities highlights where action by practitioners, program leaders, and policymakers can further improve the HSE-plus supports currently offered to opportunity youth.

NOTES

1. Marcie Foster, Julie Strawn, and Amy Ellen Duke-Benfield, *Beyond Basic Skills: State Strategies to Connect Low-Skilled Students to an Employer-Valued Postsecondary Education* (Washington, DC: Center for Law and Social Policy, 2011). Retrieved from http://www.clasp. org.

2. Mimi Corcoran, Fay Hanleybrown, Adria Steinberg, and Kate Tallant, *Collective Impact for Opportunity Youth* (Boston: FSG, 2012); Elizabeth Zachry Rutschow and Shane Crary-Ross, *Beyond the GED: Promising Models for Moving High School Dropouts to College* (New York: MDRC, January 2014).

3. John Garvey, with Terry Grobe, *From GED to College Degree: Creating Pathways to Postsecondary Success for High School Dropouts* (Boston: Jobs for the Future, May 2011); United States Government Accountability Office (February 2008).

4. Julie Nelson, *Strategies to Re-Engage Young People Not in Education, Employment or Training: A Rapid Review* (London, UK: The Centre for Excellence and Outcomes in Children and Young People's Services, 2011). Retrieved from http://archive.c4eo.org.uk/themes/youth/files/youth-rapid-review-reengage-young-people-not-in-education-employment-or-training. pdf; M. Robin Dion, *A Framework for Advancing the Well-Being and Self-Sufficiency of At-Risk Youth* (Princeton, NJ: Mathematica Policy Research, March 2013). Retrieved from http:// www.mathematica-mpr.com/~/media/publications/PDFs/family_support/YDD_framework_ IB.pdf.

5. Vanessa Martin and Joseph Broadus, *Enhancing GED Instruction to Prepare Students for College and Careers* (New York: MDRC, 2013). Retrieved from http://www.mdrc.org/sites/default/files/Enhancing_GED_Instruction_brief.pdf.

6. Foster, Strawn, and Duke-Benfield, *Beyond Basic Skills.*

7. Nelson, *Strategies to Re-Engage*; John M. Bridgeland and Jessica A Milano, *Opportunity Road: The Promise and Challenge of America's Forgotten Youth* (Washington, DC: Civic Enterprises and America's Promise Alliance, January 2012). Retrieved from http://www.dol. gov/summerjobs/pdf/OpportunityRoad.pdf.

8. Garvey, *From GED to College Degree.*
9. Martin and Broadus, *Enhancing GED Instruction.*

Chapter Sixteen

Valuing Student Voice to Inform Reengagement

Jennifer Harris and Rechelle Murillo

For at least the last decade, student voice has received recognition for its positive influence on youth development and its indirect relationship to academic achievement through increased motivation, connectedness to school, and increased agency.[1] The effects of giving voice may be even more pronounced among students who belong to vulnerable or underserved populations, including those who are homeless; those who come from the lesbian, gay, bisexual, and transgendered community; and those from racial and ethnic minority backgrounds.

Many students describe giving voice as a transformative experience, one not allowed to them previously. Facilitating student voice benefits educators as well. When adults listen to students and learn about issues in ways they would not have been capable of without the students' input, at least two benefits ensue: adults become better able to connect personally with students, and they embrace the solutions students can bring to persistent school challenges.

Taking these multiple benefits for students and caring adults into account, providing for student voice more systematically stands ready to join the ranks of common, essential elements of successful reengagement efforts. This chapter recounts one such systematic effort to gain the benefits of student voice in the context of a rapidly developing reengagement program. It also offers some initial reflections on the local benefits of tapping student voice, drawing upon the themes that emerge from student-to-student interview transcripts included here.

ADOPTING A SYSTEMATIC METHOD TO HEAR STUDENT VOICES: RENO AND THE REL

Over the past several years, leaders of the Washoe County School District (WCSD) in Reno, Nevada, have come to embrace student voice as critical to school improvement, and have set about expanding the district's capacity to engage students as partners in finding solutions to district and school challenges. The infusion of student voice within WCSD's reengagement programming and into its evaluation of reengagement efforts constitutes a strong example of the full embrace of student voice.

Reengagement in Reno

For background: The WCSD established its first Re-Engagement Centers in April 2010, through funding received from the U.S. Department of Education in the form of a five-year High School Graduation Initiative (HSGI) grant. In keeping with operating models of other reengagement centers around the United States, center staff hold responsibility for several key functions.

These functions include: locating disengaged youth; identifying student needs that affect the ability to engage in learning; providing referrals to community agencies for wraparound supports; and mentoring and advocating for students as they transition to an appropriate educational setting. Initially, WCSD opened six centers at varying locations throughout the county, some within community-based settings and some in school district facilities.

WCSD staff designed the Centers to provide caring staff who could assess needs, provide case management, and enroll students in a temporary credit recovery program in cases in which the staff needed more time to establish a permanent academic setting for the young person. Over the ensuing half decade, reengagement specialists have communicated extensively with school staff and community agencies to identify youth who have dropped out from the school system or stand at imminent risk of dropping out, make initial contact with the student and their family, and provide intensive case management to ensure students have access to support services.

A program coordinator provides supervision, training, and capacity building, and develops community partnerships that directly serve youth and their families. By the spring of 2015, the WCSD centers had served 1,699 students. Of that group, 377 had completed high school.

Reno's Approach to Embracing Student Voice

With the guidance of the Regional Education Laboratory at WestED,[2] the WCSD has adopted the definition of listening to student voice as *the practice of educators intentionally and systematically eliciting student viewpoints on a specific topic for improvement purposes.* [3] Closely attached to the definition of student voice comes the understanding that student voice experiences fall on a continuum of complexity (i.e., interactions between students and adults and resources), with higher levels of complexity associated with greater benefits to students. [4]

In turn, the level at which adult facilitators structure such experiences gets influenced by the purpose of the experience, as well as by the ability of the facilitators to commit to successful completion of a moment in practice. Exploring an issue and eliciting input constitutes the first step of a structured process to hear student voice deeply. Having formed a partnership between students and adults committed to using the structured approach together, several additional steps follow.

These steps include analysis of the information presented by the students; exploration of solutions to identified challenges; action planning; and concerted, observable actions to address the relevant challenges. Each element within the student voice process proves essential to a meaningful student voice experience. Without each of these pieces, the risk of tokenizing students grows. Going in the direction of token, unstructured student input would have the effect of devaluing student input, and could well contribute to a sense of distrust of adults among students.

Strength in Voices Conference

In June 2015, the WCSD hosted the first ever Strength in Voices conference to provide a forum for student voice, with an eye to the mission-related implications of embracing those voices—namely, increased student engagement and academic performance. District leaders, community members, and high school students across the county joined forces to create a broad spectrum of opportunities that elicited the feedback of students.

One such opportunity came in the form of a student panel that asked five students with diverse backgrounds to share their experiences while exercising their own voice within the educational setting. Students worked collaboratively with a facilitator to develop questions that would provide a snapshot of how student voice had impacted them personally.

While reflecting upon the experience of participating on the student panel, one youth who had worked her way through the reengagement process stated, "When I was in school, I didn't feel like anyone would listen or anyone would care if I left, I mean this experience is the first time I felt like I was heard." Throughout the daylong conference, students expressed the need for educators to hear students, as well as the empowerment students palpably felt when educators utilized their "voice" during the educational journey.

Tapping the voices of students in a structured manner enabled the panel to contribute to a larger district process already underway, to evaluate the antecedents of reengagement programming by exploring the conditions that had influenced student disengagement from school. In keeping with the promising practices identified with the help of REL West at WestED, district leaders sought the best understanding of the complex process of disengagement and subsequent reengagement by enlisting students as partners in exploring issues and solutions.

Student Interviews

To explore the specific local conditions that had contributed to disengagement, the WCSD also employed the Students Studying Student Stories (S4) tool from the *Speak Out, Listen Up!* Toolkit. The Toolkit provides a set of strategies for educators to plan for students' voice experiences, and had been developed in partnership between the WCSD and REL West at WestED.[5] District staff enlisted students as coresearchers to explore the issue of dropping out and persistence. Using a peer interviewing approach, several reengaged students granted interviews, so that via their peers, the district could explore why students leave the educational system and potential solutions for preventing disengagement.

Excerpts from three interviews with students who received supports and services through one of the WCSD's reengagement centers demonstrate the range of challenges students face, and provide specific student ideas for solutions to support persistence. The students confirmed that in Reno as in so many other places, varied and complex reasons lead to dropping out.

Through the interviews, students reported no less than seven preconditions for leaving school: they felt teachers didn't care about them, nor did teachers understand their personal lives; schools did not meet their individual learning needs; they fell behind in school and couldn't catch up; they had unaddressed mental health challenges, became victims of bullying, or experienced a crisis and didn't have the supports to stay on track.

Some students also revealed through the interviews reasons that they had persisted in the face of thoughts of leaving school; mainly, because they had caring teachers, coaches, and others in their lives who believed in them. Some also reported that they came to make a "choice to persist," often after a dramatic personal event in their lives, or from realizing the consequences to self and family members of not graduating.

TRANSCRIPT OF STUDENT INTERVIEWS

I: Tell me about the kind of student you were when you first started high school.

S1: When I first started high school, I was probably the student that cared, but not enough to study every night and try. I cared enough to pass. And as a freshman that is a bad idea.

S2: I can say I was like an adolescent punk. I didn't go to class. I didn't really do nothing—I just ditched every day.

S3: Better than I used to be I can say that, but still like fighting a lot and still pretty much like not as good as I wish I was.

I: Why do you think some students lose interest or drop out of school?

S1: Well, when I came to [the] Reengagement [Center] I was actually ready to drop out of school. I was ready to drop out of school because I had been bullied. I was ready to drop out because I had been pushed to the limit as far as my teachers went. In my whole life, I have had only had two teachers that cared. With certain disabilities I have, it's important that teachers listen. And teachers never listen. So, I figured getting my GED would get me further than trying to reason with teachers that didn't care. As far as other students go, they drop out because they can do it. Most people that drop out are actually of higher intelligence, not below the average IQ level. They lose interest. They don't think anyone believes in them. They feel like it's all on them, not the world around them. Which in reality is the exact opposite.

S2: Personally, it's a mix of the student's and the teachers' fault. A lot of teachers that I've noticed they don't really help. They just say, "Here's a book" and you do it yourself "and I'll go help some other people." And you get behind, pretty much fed up with it and then you just stop going.

S3: Because most of the time teachers are belittling them because of drama with other students. Because the teacher doesn't show as much effort as they should in the child's priorities.

I: Describe some of the challenges you personally experienced that made it harder for you to go to school.

S1: I have what is called schizoaffective disorder. Schizoaffective disorder is schizophrenia combined with bipolar disorder. If you know what either of those are. Schizophrenia is essentially when you become paranoid and see and hear things that are not there. Now my sophomore year, I had to be taken out of school for a year and half and do online school because of it. So I'm not entirely new to the online situation, but I've also experienced bullies because of my disorder and my weight and everything else. Students, they can be mean . . . the physical pain lasts for a little while, and the mental pain it can go on for years.

S2: Waking up every morning. How early it is; that's the hardest part. I didn't like waking up at 7 and going to school at 9.

S3: The distractions. Like with other people always trying to start some kind of drama. Always trying to talk to you while you're trying to work. Just a lot of stuff. Being dyslexic and everything and not having the teacher's support behind me also made it harder.

I: What do you like best about your current school?

S1: The fact that it's very solitary. I am not a social person for reasons given earlier in the interview, but I like doing my work alone. My little sister comes to this program and I can help her out. We usually sit side by side. She's a freshman and she needs that help that the teachers can't give, because they're tutors not teachers. They don't know the answers to everything. They don't know the answers to every single question. Even most teachers don't know those answers. I think the thing I like best here is being able to work alone and being able to do it at home because it's not like it's homework, but you're actually doing school work. You know you move further along, you do more. And it's a lot more productive in my eyes.

S2: That I can do it on my own time and the teachers actually call to say, "Hey, how are you doing? Are you going to come in today? Are you doing this? Are you doing that?" they are actually engaged with the student.

S3: The teachers they actually seem like they care other than other schools that I've been to.

I: In what ways can schools change to be more supportive of students who have experienced tough times?

S1: They need to offer support groups. I don't mean just once a week at lunch. I mean good honest support groups. If anyone was to go to Alcoholics Anonymous, they have it seven days a week. I think we need [support groups] every day of the week until issues are resolved. Because one of my social groups outside of school, we talk about this all the time. If you don't have a place to go with your issues, then you have to be your own support group, which is hard for a lot of people. I haven't been through as much as some students and I know I would benefit from a support group or one-on-one counseling or something; and they don't offer that in public schools.

S2: There's really not too many ways you can 'cause every child is different. You approach one, one way, but then it will be the wrong way to approach the next. . . . I've only been going to school for a certain amount of time. Teachers would be better to learn from students at the same time. If you had a group of teachers and a group of students come together and you all brainstormed that would probably get some progress; [if it were] just students and you seek one side, it's going to be biased either way. You have to bring together both sides.

S3: Instead of kind of being, I don't know how to describe it—like how teachers are like "Well, I don't see why you're acting like this" and doing all that and like pretty much belittling the child and everything they should sit down and try talking to them and like kind of be more of a friend in a time of need other than someone that they need to listen to constantly.

And for like teachers, is like, I think you should try understanding your students more than like trying to control them. Like don't be such a control freak. Really sit down, talk to your students. Get to know them one on one. Even if there's a lot of students, you could at least try. And that's it.

I: Okay, let's talk a little about your goals for the future now that you have moved closer to graduating. How do you feel about yourself now that you are working toward completing high school?

S1: Indifferent. I always knew I could get my diploma if I wanted to. The hardest part about it was math. I think that's a hard part for almost every student out there. It takes a certain type of person to be good at math. I feel really indifferent because it's not really something I really care to do. It's not something that I'm really passionate about. I'm not even passionate about the cap and gown ceremony. Really. I'm walking it for my mother. It's not something I'm really doing for anyone. It's not something I am doing for my family or for me. It's just something I'm doing because I'm kind of OCD about finishing stuff.

S2: I feel a lot better. When you drop out and you're not going to school. You wake up and you're just like there's nothing to do today. And then, you wake up once you're back in school and you're like well I got school to do, I got a few things to look forward to. Oh if I get this class done, that will be another credit, a good mark on my part. And then it's just like personal self-confidence. You know, if I'm back in school, it makes me feel a lot better.

S3: I feel more . . . I see more challenges ahead of me and everything, but I kind of feel more proud of myself that I'm actually getting through high school and being able to get through it. Unlike some other people, they can't get through it.

EFFECTS OF THE INTERVIEWS

Pointedly, the content of the student interviews, and subsequent activities and discussions at the conference, led the district to enact new strategies to prevent disengagement and to support students who show a determination to finish high school. Specifically, students asked for mental health services, opportunities for second chances, and personalized learning approaches to support their individual strengths and needs. Most dominant as a theme throughout the interviews: the students' demand for closer connections with their teachers and other adults in the school building.

The WCSD has taken on the task of responding to the needs brought to light by students through three principal actions. These include strengthening supports for students within the framework of multitiered systems of support; promoting restorative practices in all school buildings; and supporting students' ability to self-advocate by infusing social and emotional learning into the curriculum across all grade levels.

Washoe County's experience serves as a reminder that students want to be heard, and when given the opportunity to contribute their voice to reengagement efforts, students, practitioners, and educators, and the systems that support reengagement, can all benefit. Largely untapped at present, the full value of student voice as a reengagement tool as well as a resource for program improvement remains a new resource for districts and partners to realize.

NOTES

1. Dana Mitra, "The Significance of Students: Can Increasing Student Voice in Schools Lead to Gains in Youth Development?" *Teachers College Record* 106, no. 4, 651–88: April 2004; Dana Mitra and Steven Gross, "Increasing Student Voice in High School Reform: Building Partnerships, Improving Outcomes," *Educational Management Administration & Leadership* 37, no. 4, 522–43: July 2009.

2. "Regional Education Library," accessed October 2015, https://relwest.wested.org/.

3. BethAnn Berliner, *Utilizing Student Voice for School Improvement: A Targeted Summary of the Literature to Inform the Development of a Toolkit for District Action* (Portland, OR: Regional Educational Laboratory at WestEd, limited circulation document, unpublished, August 2012).

4. Dana Mitra, "Increasing Student Voice and Moving Toward Youth Leadership," *Prevention Researcher* 13, no. 1, 7–10: February 2006; Adam Fletcher, *Meaningful Student Involvement Guide to Students as Partners in School Change* (Bellevue, WA: HumanLinks Foundation, 2005); Eric Toshalis and Michael Nakkula, *Motivation, Engagement, and Student Voice* (Boston: Jobs for the Future Students at the Center Series, April 2012).

5. Jennifer Harris et al., *Speak Out, Listen Up! Tools for Bringing Student Ideas into School Change* (Portland, OR: U.S. Department of Education, Institute of Education Sciences, National Center for Education Evaluation and Regional Assistance, Regional Educational Laboratory West, July 2014).

Chapter Seventeen

Expanding Options such as Online and Blended Learning to Reinforce Dropout Prevention and Recovery

Lessons to Date from One School District

Tawnya Perry and Marquis Jones

One of the key challenges nationwide to supporting more students through to high school completion comes in the form of typically limited alternative options for learning and for recovering missing credits, so as to progress toward a diploma. Cities and districts that have undertaken gap analyses often find that potential demand from currently out-of-school youth who could return to some form of schooling far outstrips available alternative capacity.

In this context, the steadily increasing availability of online and blended learning tools has sparked the interest of school district officials and many others, for use at virtually all levels during the K–12 years. So, too, has the availability of specialized online and blended learning tools drawn interest among those working with struggling out-of-school youth. These specialized tools appear to hold promise as potential high-volume, low-unit-cost options.

As one part of a concerted, multipronged effort over the past decade to build alternative school capacity—which paralleled the development of reengagement capacity, detailed in chapter 10—the Los Angeles Unified School District (LAUSD) sought out and embraced online and blended learning options. Prior to this embrace, district staff witnessed daily the large-scale dropout crisis affecting the district.

LAUSD staff also became acutely aware that the district did not serve well the needs of the many students who, for various and complex reasons, left high school prior to receiving a diploma. This involved a realization that the comprehensive high school, with its traditional school hours and days, may serve many, but it clearly did not serve all.

In the process of experimenting with the expanded use of online and blended learning for struggling students and out-of-school youth, the district learned important lessons about what truly worked to boost student achievement. This chapter reviews and illustrates several key lessons, drawing upon recent experience in Los Angeles. The first lesson comes down to the observation that increasing success rates depends upon offering students more options.

A second lesson derives from paying close attention to staff selection and staff roles. Additional lessons specific to expansions in online and blended learning also emerge. What is more, the Los Angeles experience suggests the continuing lesson that resources can and perhaps will flow to efforts that can demonstrate results.

OUTSIDE THE ONE-SIZE-FITS-ALL MODEL

The 8:00 a.m. to 3:00 p.m. model of a high school on a large campus, complete with football teams and student clubs, works for many, yet certainly does not work for all. Key groups of students which Los Angeles district staff involved with online and blended learning experiments came to focus on because they needed different options included: teen mothers; children afflicted with anxiety; students working in paid employment so as to serve as the co- or sole breadwinner in a household; victims of bullying; and transient youth whose families moved frequently.

Staff determined that LAUSD needed more alternatives that would not necessarily require students to attend for six hours a day. Staff also saw a need for options through which students could complete schoolwork at home and turn in assignments once or twice each week. Staff recognized as well that some students would study better and more intensely for two or three hours each day at alternative placement locations that were conveniently located in their communities, or in the evenings at their local high schools.

LAUSD staff also found that some students successfully earned their high school diplomas through dual-credit offerings at local community college branches. In summary, the staff concluded that *raising chances for success depended upon the number of options available to students.*

EXPANDING ONLINE AND BLENDED LEARNING

One of the most intensive efforts to expand options has involved the greater use of online and blended learning. In 2007, LAUSD began implementing blended learning for credit recovery and advanced placement (AP) courses. Staff involved with dropout prevention efforts saw these tools as a currently underused but potentially very valuable resource for students who need to balance completing courses with dealing with other issues in their lives. And staff had identified numerous barriers to particular students pursuing some existing community-based credit-recovery courses.

Over time, LAUSD came to adopt two principal technology platforms to support online and blended learning at school sites: APEX and Edgenuity. As an online credit recovery system, APEX includes independent study and blended learning models. Edgenuity functions specifically as a blended learning online credit recovery program. Both programs share the goal of creating a simple way for students to recover credits. LAUSD's dropout prevention team proved instrumental for coordinating and bringing online credit recovery to targeted schools as the district implemented the two programs.

At the direct service level, the dropout prevention team laid the groundwork for use of the technology platforms by meeting with two groups of potential students: those who needed credits to catch up and get "back on track," and out-of-school youth who would benefit from developing and implementing plans for online credit recovery. The online blended courses offered flexibility for students to gain access to and complete courses in ways that fit within hectic school and personal schedules. For out-of-school youth, the online offerings provided a means to reconnect with school, and to complete courses while working or taking care of their families.

The dropout prevention team developed the special, intensive intervention of a Summer Credit Recovery Lab to make progress and expand options during the summer months. Enlisting highly qualified teachers in a concentrated setting, the summer lab received support as one activity under LAUSD's grant from the High School Graduation Initiative (HSGI) of the U.S. Department of Education. The summer lab specialized in offering the courses most often failed during the school year, and hired teachers with aligned subject matter credentials.

During the school year, dropout prevention counselors coordinated with the administrative staff at school sites to implement online blended learning courses during the school day. Several schools moved to a block schedule to accommodate the extra-long periods needed to implement the blended learning online courses within the master schedule.

This saved schools money by using auxiliary periods to implement the blended learning courses with current school staff teachers. Students could also gain access to the online courses from home or other locations where they had Internet access. For convenience, students could now also gain access to the online classes from tablets and smartphones.

For a sense of the developing scale of online and blended learning options employed at six targeted comprehensive high schools: during the 2014 to 2015 school year, ninety-three seniors completed numerous courses online and earned more than 465 credits toward graduation. During the same year, in those schools, 154 other students completed credit recovery classes and earned a total of 770 credits toward graduation.

Not all students who undertook the online and blended learning approaches completed the courses. Yet these accomplishments point out that for motivated students, the approaches provided a means to complete their current courses during the school day and complete credit recovery with convenience.

DROPOUT PREVENTION STAFF AND ADMINISTRATIVE LEADERSHIP

In addition to significantly expanded options, Los Angeles's recent experience confirms the paramount importance of selecting the right dropout prevention staff members. Complementing the description of desirable qualifications for outreach workers in chapter 8 in this volume, LAUSD identified several essential specifications and qualities for in-district personnel.

For instance, the most effective efforts of a district dropout prevention specialist often occur outside the traditional school hours. Home visits occur frequently, especially for students who have already left school. Resilience constitutes a critical quality, and patience a critical attitude. The ability to apply creativity to reestablish effective relationships with parents and students and create student pathways to success comes in handy each day.

Within major roles that include supporting the front-line staff and relating to higher-up officials, Los Angeles's experience suggests several specific tasks for an effective district-level dropout prevention administrator. One key task: continuously acknowledging and rewarding staff through emotionally trying circumstances. LAUSD's administrator has found it effective to provide public recognition at staff professional development meetings and in program or school newsletters, and to distribute certificates to staff with particularly high success rates of student achievement.

The dropout prevention administrator must also provide oversight of the program and maintain communication with representatives of external funding sources. Other key contacts for regular communication include district-level administrators and the school site administrators—principals or assistant principals. Experience shows that school administrators at all levels want to see the data that shows decreases in dropout rates and improvement in graduation rates.

RESOURCES FOLLOW SUCCESS

Efforts to expand dropout prevention and recovery options in LAUSD—such as the expansion of useful online and blended learning options—have relied upon several different funding sources over the past decade, and have won continued and sometimes expanded funding as a result of notable successes. Initial funding from the LAUSD Office of Instruction supported efforts for the first three years, beginning in 2006. When district-level funding subsided, some middle school and high school principals supported dedicated dropout prevention staff positions from within the school-level budget.

In the 2009 to 2010 school year, LAUSD became one of twenty-six school districts nationwide to receive support for dropout prevention and recovery from the U.S. Department of Education in the form of a five-year High School Graduation Initiative grant. As federal funding came to an end in 2015, with no option of grant renewal, district officials determined to fund, and indeed to expand, services available in twelve schools that have served as the primary locus of prevention and online/blended learning activity. LAUSD has also committed to increase the number of school sites involved to thirty-nine.

A decade's worth of experience in staffing for dropout prevention and recovery, and adopting online and blended learning approaches to expand high school completion options, conveys helpful lessons from one of the nation's largest school districts applicable in districts of all sizes. Carefully selecting and supporting staff and expanding options have paid off as one element of the Los Angeles strategy.

Chapter Eighteen

Future Prospects

Andrew O. Moore

The Reengagement Network to which so many authors have given voice in this volume has grown steadily in size and scope since its inception in 2011. The variety of views, accomplishments, and challenges the authors describe also help inform a reflective moment to consider future prospects for reengagement. Indeed, a sketch of opportunities and challenges on the near and farther horizons encompasses several topics: a range of items in the broad policy category; peer learning; and the closely interrelated topics of program replication and evaluation.

POLICY TO ADVANCE AND UNDERGIRD REENGAGEMENT

A range of policy-level developments, at the city, school district, state, and national levels, could advance and undergird reengagement. Left unchanged, some aspects of current policy will have an opposite, braking effect. An even more intentional adoption of a policy agenda on the part of the Reengagement Network could lead to priority setting, so as to seize opportunities and reduce or eliminate barriers. Setting the overall course toward the goal of spreading reengagement programs to every city and town in the nation would help as well.

City and School District

Recognizing the need to fill the reengagement niche and committing resources to operate a reengagement center or program remains a rare step across the national landscape. City leaders can defuse potential tensions by adopting a share of the responsibility for responding to local dropout patterns, and can reach out to enlist elected and appointed school leaders who may otherwise fill their time responding to the needs of students still attending school. Fostering productive local conversations about how to fill the niche must remain a priority for reengagement approaches to spread much further.

City leaders can also follow the lead of Reengage Phoenix to enlist city departments, such as libraries, to host reengagement efforts; leverage their appointments to local Workforce Boards to influence policy, emphasis, and funding; steer or raise resources to staff reengagement programs; and fold attention to integrating out-of-school youth into the workforce into local plans, policies, and expenditures for economic development.

Also, as noted at multiple points throughout this volume, in order for reengagement efforts to offer a sufficient supply of education options for returning students, school districts (and charter schools as local education agencies of their own) must reconceptualize and grow these options significantly. Rare indeed is the locality with a 20 percent dropout rate, where 20 percent of seats for completing high school operate along the alternative continuum. Adopting this new standard—based on the *total number of young residents who could benefit* from services and supports to complete high school, rather than the *number still enrolled*—must become the norm.

State Policy

With states as the ultimate drivers of education policy, it becomes essential to consider the ways that state policy affects the growth or limitations of local reengagement efforts. For instance, the Network has witnessed the advent, and recognized the availability, of policy in at least four states—Illinois, Iowa, Texas, and Washington—that supplies additional state resources to the local level. (In a rather different setting, Washington, D.C., also mustered funds from its budget to underwrite reengagement center startup.) Four out of fifty represents a beachhead, but hardly a critical mass. What would it take for more states to get on board?

One answer may rest with a current trend in which states adopt a higher compulsory education age, often as high as eighteen. In Kentucky, for instance, school districts' widespread adoption of the higher age creates a market for reengagement. Yet the fulfillment of the promise will only occur if the state and districts unpack the implications of the new law in terms of services, supports, and accountability regimes.

Indeed, a small number of other states have altered, or may alter, accountability rules in favor of reenrolling out-of-school youth. In Massachusetts, reengagement now stands as a positive factor in the statewide accountability system for high schools. Removing the perverse disincentives that most districts nationwide now face to reenrolling former dropouts thus emerges as a priority in order for districts even to consider playing a role. Such disincentives most commonly take the form of achievement calculations that do not readily account for, and sometimes penalize schools and districts for, helping dropouts resume their education.

One new development at the state level could provide a means to address the need for policy change (or at least inform policy), while also ensuring more peer support for operations. In 2015, Colorado established the first statewide Reengagement Network. The primary purpose of this network: provide mutual support, and streamline coordination of regional and state-wide student reengagement efforts. State network organizers with Colorado Youth for a Change, drawing some initial support from the state Department of Education, seek to engender a collaborative environment that increases capacity and improves the quality of reengagement efforts.

Similarly, with only light staffing at the state level, the Washington Office of the Superintendent of Public Instruction (OSPI) has regularly convened Open Doors (http://www.k12.wa.us/GATE/SupportingStudents/StudentRetrieval.aspx) sites from across the state. OSPI also maintains an "open book" style website with proceedings of the cross-site meetings available for viewing, and numerous procedural documents available for download. As the sponsor of the largest concentration of reengagement efforts in one state—three dozen and counting—OSPI provides one good model for keeping sites connected, which other states with multiple reengagement sites could readily adapt.

Federal Policy

Unresolved ongoing debates about the best role for the federal government in education contribute to a less definite picture regarding the potential contributions of national policy to advance reengagement. New workforce legislation specifically naming dropout recovery as an allowable activity stands in contrast to the lack of a secure foothold in education legislation and funding. The latter condition may bespeak a lack of concerted advocacy, or the continued "too big to be seen" invisibility of the out-of-school youth population.

Indeed, three recent disappointments also serve to suggest possible future directions for federal education policy regarding reengagement. The nonrenewal of High School Graduation Initiative grants, after five years of funding at a record-high level totaling $50 million, erased a much-needed direct line of dropout prevention and recovery support from the U.S. Department of Education to districts. Reinstating such direct support, even at a pilot level, would put the federal shoulder to the wheel to spread reengagement.

In a second disappointment, congressional staff came to view adding a plank to omnibus education legislation specific to dropout recovery as "a bridge too far" as the legislative process advanced in 2015. Representatives of the field and their elected representatives must now identify other opportunities to provide reengagement with the crucial piece of authorizing legislation that confers legitimacy in subsequent policy and appropriations processes.

And in a third missed opportunity, recent efforts to spur innovation from the federal level have not encouraged applications from the alternative education and reengagement arena. To the degree the U.S. Department of Education or other agencies continue to adopt this policy-leading, incentivizing-reform strategy, they would do well to ensure that out-of-school youth stand to benefit at least in proportion to their numbers in the population—and perhaps more, to drive federal resources to such youth as a high-need group.

On the other hand, the 2014 passage and 2015 onward implementation of the Workforce Innovation and Opportunity Act (WIOA) may send important proreengagement signals and spur new local activity. WIOA includes a requirement to spend 75 percent of locally managed youth-training funds on out-of-school youth, and for the first time names dropout recovery as an allowable activity. Whereas the overall bill asks local agencies to do more with the same or less funding, the reordering of priorities and concentration on the out-of-school population appear as steps in the right direction.

SUPPORTING ONGOING PEER LEARNING

Based on the active participation of scores of professionals in so many facets of the Reengagement Network, including this book, momentum appears very strong to sustain a high level of peer and cross-site learning. The Network has turned a corner, beyond the days when minimal staffing proved sufficient for essential roles such as promoting and maintaining contact among Network members, curating information, getting questions answered, and organizing in-person meetings. More intensive staffing has become a must, even as volunteer task forces undertake short-term projects and communications technology helps at the margin.

With interest growing, and without losing the "all-in" spirit of the Network—through which, for instance, small groups of volunteers produced four national conferences in Decembers 2011 through 2014 like clockwork—formalizing key structures and functions rises to the top of the agenda. Recognizing and building upon multiple overlaps of topical interest and mission among the Network and other players in the youth employment and alternative education fields provides one possible avenue. Identifying new financing methods and philanthropic partners provides another. The next years of the Network will include sorting and choosing new operating options.

EVALUATION, REPLICABILITY, SUSTAINABILITY

Interrelated with policy and operating structures, how to sustain, grow, and understand the contributions of individual reengagement programs and the Network as a whole rises as a third major topic at this turning point for the field. Of note, amid calls for "evidence-based practices" and "collective impact," reengagement has moved forward as an important area for piloting and experimentation, thankfully insulated from immediate demands for rigorous proof of effectiveness and efficiency. Indeed, reengagement centers initially drew the National League of Cities' interest as one example among several of emerging cross-system collaborations.

Having found the operating space for initial experimentation brings with it the fragility and limits to growth that affect many boutique social policy developments. Some—but fortunately not all—of the initial progress of spreading and growing reengagement has relied more on the passion of key individuals than upon policy. And the field has yet to benefit from research and evaluation to understand causal links and correlations fully. It becomes hard to imagine the kind of quantum growth necessary to reach millions of out-of-school youth without first obtaining independent documentation of what works, and why.

The time has arrived, then, for more experienced reengagement sites to develop partnerships with interested researchers and evaluators. Studies along the full continuum from formative to impact evaluation could begin posthaste, thanks in part to the commitment to gathering administrative data that several chapters in this volume exemplify. Philanthropic partners and others must add evaluation to the list of near-term priority reengagement investments and deployments of resources—perhaps in the context of support for a multisite replication or scaling effort.

As examples of potential research and evaluation partners, some regional education laboratories and evaluation firms could open areas of concentration focused on reengagement. University-based researchers nearby current reengagement nodes will find ample angles for inquiry. Regional Federal Reserve Bank branches committed to understanding all aspects of workforce development could undertake research, paralleling the contributions such banks have made to illuminate the benefits of early childhood education. A wave of action research involving practitioners and youth would help as well.

The future prospects for an expanded, sustainable reengagement field shine brightly against the backdrop of the nationwide and local needs of a still largely unrecognized population. Adopting an audacious goal—a reengagement center in every community—could provide the necessary vision. To bring that vision to reality, attending to policy, peer learning and support, and program evaluation remains the best formula for further success.

Resources and References

National League of Cities Institute for Youth, Education, and Families

NLC makes a variety of resources available to city officials exploring options for creating a reengagement center or program for out-of-school youth:

- The NLC Dropout Reengagement Network welcomes new members as well as requests for information or assistance. The Network meets several times per year via conference call and once each year in person. In support of the Network, NLC curates an online reengagement programs folder available on the Web. Network members and NLC staff regularly post new and relevant examples, articles, and policies. To learn more about the Network or to gain access to the additional resources on the Web, contact Andrew Moore at Moore@nlc.org.
- NLC's reengagement web page includes links to reports and webinars on reengagement initiatives: http://www.nlc.org/reengagement/.
- The NLC blog—CitiesSpeak—regularly offers the latest look at reengagement efforts around the country: http://citiesspeak.org/author/andrewomoore/.

U.S. Department of Education

Rennie-Hill, Leslie, Jenni Villano, Michelle Feist, Nettie Legters, Jean Thomases, and Patrice Williams. *Bringing Students Back to the Center: A Resource Guide for Implementing and Enhancing Re-Engagement Centers for Out-of-School Youth.* U.S. Department of Education: The Millennium Group, November 2014.

U.S. Department of Education. "High School Graduation Initiative." Last modified August
2014. http://www2.ed.gov/programs/dropout/index.html.

Center for Labor Markets and Policy, Drexel University

The Center for Labor Markets and Policy is the hub for applied research and technical consult-
ing for human resource development issues at Drexel University.
Drexel University. "Center for Labor Markets and Policy." Accessed October 2015. http://
www.drexel.edu/clmp/.

Center for Promise, America's Promise Alliance

The Center for Promise, the research institute at America's Promise Alliance, identifies the
needs of young people and shares strategies to meet those needs.
Center for Promise. *Back to School: Exploring Promising Practice for Re-Engaging Young
People in Secondary Education.* America's Promise Alliance, December 2014.
Center for Promise. *Dispelling Stereotypes of Young People Who Leave School before Gradua-
tion.* America's Promise Alliance, August 2015.
Center for Promise. *Don't Call Them Dropouts: Understanding the Experiences of Young
People That Leave High School before Graduation.* America's Promise Alliance, May 2014.
Hynes, Michelle. *Don't Quit on Me: What Young People Who Left School Say about the Power
of Relationships.* Center for Promise, America's Promise Alliance, September 2015.
Swanson, Christopher. *Cities in Crisis 2009: Closing the Graduation Gap.* America's Promise
Alliance: Editorial Projects in Education Research Center, April 2009.

The Rennie Center for Education Research & Policy

The Rennie Center strives to improve public education by creating a platform and developing
resources for educators and policymakers to make well-informed decisions.
Culbertson, Nina, Jennifer Poulos, and Chad d'Entremont. *Creating Pathways to Success for
Opportunity Youth: Lessons from Three Massachusetts Communities.* Rennie Center for
Education Research & Policy, November 2014.
d'Entremont, Chad, and Nina Zockoff. *Forgotten Youth: Re-Engaging Students through Drop-
out Recovery.* Rennie Center for Education Research & Policy, November 2012.
Poulos, Jennifer, Chad d'Entremont, and Nina Culbertson. *Youth Transition Task Force: A
Ten-Year Retrospective.* Rennie Center for Education Research & Policy, April 2015.

Jobs for the Future/Back on Track through College

Jobs for the Future's Back on Track through College model aims to reengage youth and young
adults who are off track to graduation—or disconnected from both education and work—
and puts them on a path to postsecondary credentials.
Allen, Lili, and Rebecca Wolfe. *Back on Track to College: A Texas School District Leverages
State Policy to Put Dropouts on the Path to Success.* Jobs for the Future, September 2010.
Jobs for the Future. "Reengaging Opportunity Youth." Accessed October 2015. http://www.jff.
org/initiatives/back-track-designs/.

Civic Enterprises

Civic Enterprises is a public policy and strategy firm that specializes in research and policy
development.
Belfield, Clive, Henry Levin, and Rachel Rosen. *The Economic Value of Opportunity Youth.*
Civic Enterprises, January 2012.

Bridgeland, John, John Dilulio, and Karen Morison. *The Silent Epidemic: Perspectives of High School Dropouts*. Civic Enterprises in association with Peter D. Hart Research Associates for the Bill & Melinda Gates Foundation, March 2006.

DePaoli, Jennifer, Joanna Fox, Erin Ingram, Mary Maushard, John Bridgeland, and Robert Balfanz. *Building a Grad Nation: Progress and Challenge in Ending the High School Dropout Epidemic*. Civic Enterprises: Everyone Graduates Center at Johns Hopkins University, May 2015.

OTHER USEFUL RESOURCES ON REENGAGEMENT

Reports

Annie E. Casey Foundation. *Youth and Work: Restoring Teen and Young Adult Connections to Opportunity*. Annie E. Casey Foundation, March 2012.

Burd-Sharps, Sarah, and Kristen Lewis. *One in Seven: Ranking Youth Disconnection in the 25 Largest Metro Areas*. Measure of America, Social Science Research Council, September 2014.

Education Week. Diplomas Count 2013: Turning Dropouts into Graduates. Education Week and Editorial Projects in Education, June 2013.

Fernandes-Alcantara, Adrienne. *Disconnected Youth: A Look at 16 to 24 Year Olds Who Are Not Working or in School*. Congressional Research Service, October 2015.

Government Accountability Office. *Disconnected Youth: Federal Action Could Address Some of the Challenges Faced by Local Programs That Reconnect Youth to Education and Employment*. Government Accountability Office, February 2008.

Reyna, Ryan. *State Policies to Reengage Dropouts*. NGA Center for Best Practices, July 2011.

Sources of Ongoing Practice Support and Reports from the Field

Alternative Schools Network. "Alternative Schools Network: Creating Futures Every Day." Accessed October 2015. www.asnchicago.org/.

American Youth Policy Forum. "Dropout Prevention and Recovery." Accessed October 2015. http://www.aypf.org/programareas/dropout-prevention-and-recovery/.

Community Service Society of New York. "Opportunities for Youth." Accessed October 2015. http://www.cssny.org/issues/entry/opportunities-for-youth/.

Gevirtz Graduate School of Education, UC Santa Barbara. "California Dropout Research Project." Last modified July 2015. http://www.cdrp.ucsb.edu/.

John Hopkins University, School of Education. "Everyone Graduates Center." Accessed October 2015. http://every1graduates.org/.

MDC, Inc. "Our Projects: Made in Durham." Accessed October 2015. http://www.mdcinc.org/projects/made-durham/.

MDRC. "Population: Populations with Barriers to Employment." Accessed October 2015. http://www.mdrc.org/population/focus/high-school-dropouts/.

National Youth Employment Coalition. "Home." Accessed October 2015. www.nyec.org/.

Youth Transition Funders Group. "Multiple Pathways to Graduation Work Group." Accessed October 2015. http://ytfg.org/multiple-pathways-to-graduation-work-group/.

BIBLIOGRAPHY FOR SELECTED CHAPTERS

Chapter 5: Reengagement in Boston: Changing the Conversation and Driving Dropout Reduction

"Dropping Back In." *Boston Globe*, April 2007.

Jan, Tracy. "Dropout Is Now In, Lesson Learned." *Boston Globe*, September 8, 2006.

"Outreach for Dropouts." *Boston Globe*, February 13, 2005.

"Small Programs Yield Big Results for At-Risk Students." *Boston Globe*, February 12, 2015.

Hamilton, Kathy, Neil Sullivan, Andrew Bundy, and Lainy Fersh. *Too Big to Be Seen: The Invisible Dropout Crisis in Boston and America.* Boston Youth Transitions Task Force, May 2006.

Khatiwada, Ishwar, Joseph McLaughlin, and Andrew Sum. *The Fiscal Economic Consequences of Dropping Out of High School.* Center for Labor Market Studies, Northeastern University, January 2007.

Khatiwada, Ishwar, Joseph McLaughlin, and Andrew Sum. Young High School Dropouts in Boston: A Profile of Their Demographic and Socioeconomic Characteristics and Their Labor Market Experiences and Problems. Center for Labor Market Studies, Northeastern University, October 2005.

Office of Data and Accountability. Impact of Credit Recovery Program on the 2012 4-Year Graduation Rate. Boston Public Schools, October 2012.

Office of Data and Accountability. Q and A Boston Public Schools 2013–2014: Student Dropout Rates. Boston Public Schools, January 2015.

The Parthenon Group. *Strategic Planning to Serve Off-Track Youth: Data Review and Strategic Implications.* The Parthenon Group, September 2007.

Research and Evaluation Group, UMass Donahue Institute. Boston Public Schools 2010–2011 Credit Skills Recovery Program (CSRP) Summary of Findings. UMass Donahue Institute, January 2012.

Chapter 10: Effectively Leveraging Institutional and Community Partnerships: Examples from Los Angeles and Nashville

City of Los Angeles Workforce Investment Board. *Workforce Innovation Fund Application: LA Reconnections Career Academy (LARCA).* U.S. Department of Labor, March 2012.http://webapps.dol.gov/DOLGrantData/GrantInformation.aspx?appid=13997/.

Dickson, Alison, Neeta Fogg, Paul Harrington, and Ishwar Khatiwada. *The Lifetime Employment, Earnings and Poverty Consequences of Dropping Out of High School in the Los Angeles Metro Area.* Center for Labor Market Studies, Northeastern University, October 2009.

Fogg, Neeta, and Paul Harrington. *The Teen Disconnection in Los Angeles and Its Neighborhoods.* Center for Labor Market Studies, Northeastern University, November 2004.

Harrington, Paul, Neeta Fogg, and Alison Dickson. *The Fiscal Consequences of Dropping Out of High School in the Los Angeles Metro Area.* Center for Labor Market Studies, Northeastern University, June 2010.

Los Angeles County Economic Development Corporation. *Los Angeles County: Strategic Plan for Economic Development.* Los Angeles County Economic Development Corporation, December 2009.

UNITE-LA. *LA Compact.* Los Angeles Regional Chamber of Commerce: UNITE-LA, February 2010.

Chapter 16: Valuing Student Voice to Inform Reengagement

Berliner, BethAnn. *Utilizing Student Voice for School Improvement: A Targeted Summary of the Literature to Inform the Development of a Toolkit for District Action.* Portland, OR: Regional Educational Laboratory at WestEd. Limited circulation document, unpublished. August 2012.

Fletcher, Adam. *Meaningful Student Involvement Guide to Students as Partners in School Change.* Bellevue, WA: HumanLinks Foundation, 2005.

Harris, Jennifer, Laura Davidson, Ben Hayes, Kelly Humphreys, Paul LaMarca, BethAnn Berliner, Leslie Poynor, and Lori Van Houten. *Speak Out, Listen Up! Tools for Using Student Perspectives and Local Data for School Improvement.* Portland, OR: U.S. Department of Education, Institute of Education Sciences, National Center for Education Evaluation and Regional Assistance, Regional Educational Laboratory West, July 2014.

Mitra, Dana. "Increasing Student Voice and Moving Toward Youth Leadership." *Prevention Researcher* 13, no. 1, 7–10: February 2006.

Mitra, Dana. "The Significance of Students: Can Increasing Student Voice in Schools Lead to Gains in Youth Development?" *Teachers College Record* 106, no. 4: 651–88: April 2004.

Mitra, Dana, and Steven Gross. "Increasing Student Voice in High School Reform: Building Partnerships, Improving Outcomes." *Educational Management Administration & Leadership* 37, no. 4: 522–43: July 2009. DOI: 10.1177/1741143209334577.

Toshalis, Eric, and Michael Nakkula. *Motivation, Engagement, and Student Voice*. Boston: Jobs for the Future Students at the Center Series, April 2012.

Index

About the Editor

Andrew O. Moore is the director for Youth and Young Adult Connections at the National League of Cities Institute for Youth, Education, and Families in Washington, D.C. Moore leads a broad program area at the YEF Institute, a foundation-funded "action tank" that helps municipal leaders take action on behalf of the children, youth, and families in their communities. Current areas of focus, in addition to support for the Reengagement Network, include municipal leadership for juvenile justice and jail reform, connecting children to nature, and Pay for Success financing.

During and prior to his time with the Institute, Moore has written and published extensively on youth development topics. Earlier, he spent fifteen years building the nationwide network of service and conservation corps, and he has consulted on strategic program development with multiple clients in the youth development field in the United States and United Kingdom. Moore holds degrees from Princeton University and the University of Pennsylvania's Fels Institute of Government, and he served as an Atlantic Fellow in Public Policy in the United Kingdom from 2000 to 2001. He serves on the boards of the National Youth Employment Coalition and Conservation Legacy.

About the Contributors

Emmanuel Allen, Dropout Recovery Specialist, Boston Private Industry Council, Boston, Massachusetts. As a lifelong Boston resident, Emmanuel Allen is dedicated to the success and achievement of urban youth. For the past fourteen years, he has worked to create programming and pathways for a wide variety of youth ranging from homeless, high school dropouts and the at-risk to first-year college students. Emmanuel helped design the Boston Public Schools Re-Engagement Center, a full service center that actively recovers students who have left school. He also managed and organized programs targeted toward reducing violence in urban areas.

Emmanuel holds a Bachelor of Science from Fitchburg State University in Computer Information Systems, and a certificate in Nonprofit Leadership and Management from Boston University. He is an MBA candidate at Northeastern University.

Glen Biggs, Senior Associate Director, Alignment Nashville, Nashville, Tennessee. Glen began his career working with youth-serving organizations at the Oasis Center in Nashville in 1995. In his daily work with Alignment, Glen coaches and facilitates local teams of community leaders in developing tactics that bring about systems change. Alignment's purpose is to strategically and systemically align community organizations and their resources in support of public education, children's health, and college and career readiness. Glen and the 16–24 Out of School, Out of Work team have been working on the issues related to the Opportunity Youth of Nashville and reengagement since 2009.

Glen holds a BSBA from Aquinas College. He is a certified Life and Leadership Coach (NLPC), a member of the Institute for Cultural Affairs (ICA), and serves on the Education Council for the Frist Center for the Visual Arts.

Nina Culbertson, Senior Research Associate, Rennie Center for Education Research & Policy, Boston, Massachusetts. Nina Culbertson works to improve public education through well-informed decision making based on a deep knowledge of evidence of effective policymaking and practice. As the senior research associate, she leads research efforts related to dropout prevention and recovery, alternative education, student mobility, teacher preparation, and school budgeting, among other topics. All research projects seek to promote an education system that provides every child with the opportunity to be successful in school and in life.

Nina joined the Rennie Center with a background in international education research, having worked at the Trends in International Mathematics and Science Study and the Progress in Reading Literacy Study (TIMSS & PIRLS). She began her education career supporting the headmaster of a full-service school in Boston, and has served as a developmental instructor for college students. Nina holds a Master of Education in Education Research, Measurement, and Evaluation and a Bachelor of Arts in Human Development, both from Boston College.

Jennifer L. Danese, Vice President of Operations, Communities in Schools, Lehigh Valley, Pennsylvania. Jennifer L. Danese oversees programs and services in five school districts in Pennsylvania. She has experience working with a wide range of students, including those living in poverty. Jennifer strives to help all individuals create, become, and realize their best selves and greatest potential. She is a graduate of The Pennsylvania State University, where she earned her master's in education, and St. Joseph's University, where she earned her bachelor's in psychology. Jennifer is a Certified School Counselor and National Certified Counselor. She has a loving and supportive family.

Dr. Chad d'Entremont, Executive Director, Rennie Center for Education Research & Policy, Boston, Massachusetts. Dr. Chad d'Entremont shepherds the Rennie Center's mission to ensure education decision making is based on deep knowledge and evidence of effective policymaking and practice. In this capacity, he coauthored numerous articles and reports on strategies to support all students in graduating from high school, accessing postsecondary education, and achieving sustained life success. He has a PhD in Education Policy and Social Analysis and a master's in the Sociology of Education from Teachers College, Columbia University.

Dr. d'Entremont oversaw the launch of the Massachusetts Institute for College and Career Readiness (MICCR) in partnership with the Boston University School of Education and MassINC. The MICCR team works with low-income, urban school districts to design, implement, and evaluate programming to enhance college and career readiness. Dr. d'Entremont began his career as a teacher, serving high-needs students. He was the former assistant director of a nationally renowned research center at Teachers College, Columbia University, and, from 2007 to 2011, he was the research and policy director at Strategies for Children.

Steve Dobo, Founder and CEO, Zero Dropouts, Denver, Colorado. Steve Dobo is a nationally known practitioner, author, presenter, and researcher in the field of education and dropout reengagement. Zero Dropouts is an educational social enterprise based in Denver and is committed to all students succeeding in education and life. Steve consults with school districts across the country to improve high school graduation and dropout rates, and with colleges to increase postsecondary success rates. Steve blends his unique background in science, math, data, and technology with his expertise in counseling to approach his work in both a research- and relationship-based way.

Steve has worked extensively with homeless teens and families and parents in poverty and youth at risk of education failure across the country in various settings, including municipal government, school districts, and non-profit organizations. Steve earned his bachelor's degree in physics from the University of North Carolina at Chapel Hill and his master's of education in counseling from Colorado State University.

Dr. Debra Duardo, Executive Director of Student Health and Human Services, Los Angeles Unified School District, Los Angeles, California. Debra Duardo is responsible for the administrative oversight of support services and district programs including Student Medical Services, School Nursing, School Mental Health, Pupil Services, Dropout Prevention and Recovery, Community Partners, and Medi-Cal programs. Her unique life experience as a high school dropout able to overcome obstacles and rise to the position of executive director drives her passion to ensure that all students receive an education in a safe, caring environment and that every student is college prepared and career ready.

A 2014 to 2015 Stanton Fellow from the Durfee Foundation, Dr. Duardo's goal is to engage parents and guardians of students to decrease chronic absenteeism from kindergarten through the twelfth grade, a strong predictor of high school dropout. Dr. Duardo holds a master's degree in social work from the University of California, Los Angeles (UCLA), and a doctorate from UCLA's Graduate School of Education and Information Studies. Appointed by former Los Angeles mayor Antonio Villaraigosa, she also served as a city commissioner on the Commission for Community and Family Services.

Celine Fejeran, Senior Director for Strategic Initiatives, Raise DC, Washington, D.C. Celine spearheads the Graduation Pathways Project, a cross-sector effort to improve citywide high school outcomes through supporting the adoption of impactful practices for programs serving youth who are off track to graduation, expanding "second chance" opportunities for reconnecting youth, and developing key policies to advance these efforts. She has a master's degree in Education Policy from George Washington University and a bachelor's degree in elementary education from American University.

Prior to joining the Raise DC team, Celine served as a senior policy advisor in the District of Columbia Office of the Deputy Mayor for Education, where she cofounded DC's first youth Re-Engagement Center and executed an unprecedented diagnostic of the city's dropout population across both DC public schools and public charter schools. Celine also has served as a policy analyst for the DC Alliance of Youth Advocates, where she collaborated with nonprofits, government agencies, and elected officials to enhance workforce development opportunities for young people.

Heather Ficht, Executive Director, East Cascades Workforce Investment Board, and former Director of Youth Workforce Services, Worksystems, Portland, Oregon. Heather Ficht managed Worksystems's youth workforce programs and investments and ensured coordination and alignment with other systems, including the Department of Human Services, K–12 schools, community colleges, and local governments. Heather joined Worksystems in 2005. She has twelve years of experience working with youth who are homeless and/or have a criminal background, and she served as a school social worker in East Multnomah County. She serves on the Cradle to Career Steering Committee and the Oregon Career Information System's Board.

Heather received her bachelor's in sociology from University of Wisconsin-Madison and a master's in social work from Portland State University.

Carla Gay, Administrator of Reconnection Services, Multiple Pathways to Graduation at Portland Public Schools, Portland, Oregon. Carla Gay began her career as a teacher in Nevada, working as a reading specialist with elementary-age students and struggling high school students. After spending some time living in Africa, she returned to earn her Master of Social Work degree with an emphasis in social and economic development from Washington University in St. Louis, Missouri, and an initial administrator's license from Portland State University. She studied Spanish in Central America and then settled in Portland, Oregon, to begin working with at-risk young people in the education field.

Carla has nearly twenty years of experience working with students who have disengaged from school before completing their secondary education. She currently oversees all of the reengagement efforts for disconnected youth who reside in Portland public school boundaries. She is passionate about building equitable education systems that offer a range of rigorous, engaging programming for *all* students so they feel welcome, wanted, and worthy of a quality learning experience. Carla enjoys spending time with her family, playing in the outdoors, reading, and traveling. She lives with her wife and their two children.

Kathy Hamilton, Youth Transitions Director, Boston Private Industry Council, Boston, Massachusetts. Kathy serves as the youth transitions director at the Boston Private Industry Council (PIC), Boston's Workforce Development Board, and school-to-career intermediary. Kathy works to build education and career pathways for young adults as part of the PIC's broader convening efforts. Over the last ten years, she has organized the Youth Transitions Task Force to focus Boston on reducing its high school dropout rate. Kathy helped found the Boston Re-Engagement Center, which has reenrolled dropouts into the Boston public schools since 2009.

Kathy helps to convene Boston's Opportunity Youth Collaborative. She also leads the PIC postsecondary team, which provides coaching services for urban, first-generation college students. She participates actively in several national networks, including the National Youth Employment Coalition, the ReEngagement Network, and the Intermediary Network. A graduate of Hampshire College, Kathy has collaborated on a number of research and policy reports, including "Too Big to Be Seen: The Dropout Crisis in Boston and America," a 2006 primer on the dropout challenge.

Jennifer Harris, Program Evaluator, Washoe County School District (WCSD), Reno, Nevada. Jennifer Harris earned her Bachelor of Arts in Psychology and Sociology at California State University at Chico and her Masters in Applied Sociology at Northern Arizona University. As program evaluator, she collaborates with program leaders to establish program objectives, create comprehensive evaluation plans, carry out data collection strategies, analyze data, and communicate evaluation findings to various audience groups. Her primary responsibilities include developing and implementing evaluation projects that inform the work of dropout prevention and reengagement efforts in the WCSD.

Ms. Harris is currently engaged in examining districtwide systems and services that influence the enrollment patterns of students with disabilities. Ms. Harris supports WCSD's effort to promote success for all students through building authentic student voice opportunities for students to contribute solutions to persistent school challenges. In collaboration with other champions of student voice, her efforts have led to: the creation of the Speak Out, Listen Up! Toolkit; the formation of a district-level committee on student voice; training sessions for educators; the first annual Student Data Symposium; and the first annual Student Voice Summit.

Shirley Horstman, Director of Student Services, Dubuque Community Schools, Dubuque, Iowa. Growing up, Shirley's parents always emphasized the importance of education. They expected all of their children to graduate from college. Neither one of her parents had the opportunity to even attend high school. After graduating from Loras College in Dubuque, Iowa, she began her career as a high school mathematics teacher at Boylan Central Catholic High School in Rockford, Illinois. Her teaching career continued in the small northwestern Illinois community of East Dubuque, where she taught both middle and high school students.

Upon completing a master's degree in educational technology, she became the mathematics facilitator at Keystone Area Education Agency, overseeing twenty-six school districts in northeast Iowa. Shirley joined Dubuque Community Schools as the mathematics and science supervisor. She is now their director of student services. In her current role, Shirley is able to work with at-risk youth to remove barriers to completing high school. She has also been an adjunct mathematics professor at Clarke (College) University. She is a member of the East Dubuque School Board.

Marquis Jones, Extended Learning Academy Counselor, Fremont High School, Los Angeles, California. Marquis Jones brings a background in youth services to his current role as administrator for the Group Home Scholars Program, which serves all of the students within the Los Angeles Unified School District who reside in a group home. Jones's earlier experience includes serving as an academic counselor and diploma project counselor, including with the team that raised Fremont High School's graduation rate from 37.7 percent to 68 percent. He subsequently served as lead counselor with the LAUSD Diploma Project.

Jones graduated from California State University-Northridge with a BS in sociology and a minor in criminology and corrections. He earned a master's degree in educational counseling from National University in 2004. In recent years, he has served as a regular presenter in workshops at The COBA Scholarship Conference, and also for Los Angeles Skills Builders Unlimited, Cash for College, the School Social Work Association of America, and the National At-Risk Youth Conference. In his spare time, Marquis enjoys riding motorcycles and dirt bikes, snowboarding, mountain biking (off trail), paintball wars, working out, and mainly, playing with his children.

Nick Mathern, Associate Vice President, Policy & Partnership Development, Gateway to College, Portland, Oregon. Nick Mathern is associate vice president of policy and partnership development for Gateway to College

National Network. Since 2005, he has brokered agreements between colleges, school districts, and state education agencies to replicate and implement Gateway to College programs in more than fifty communities. Nick is responsible for developing and executing the National Network's policy agenda, which aims to broaden pathways and create appropriate funding and accountability systems for opportunity youth to reengage with education and achieve postsecondary success.

Before coming to Gateway, Nick taught in a small alternative high school. Nick's previous career was in social services, involving child abuse intervention, serving children and families who were survivors of domestic violence, and working with adjudicated youth and adults. He holds a Bachelor of Arts in Sociology from Drake University and a master's in public administration with a focus on education policy from the Hatfield School of Government at Portland State University.

Rechelle Murillo, Unity Coordinator/Social Worker, Washoe County School District, Reno, Nevada. Rechelle Murillo has overseen the reengagement efforts of the Washoe County School District (WCSD) in Reno, Nevada, for the past five years. She currently serves as the unity coordinator and is responsible for coordinating the truancy intervention and reengagement programs for WCSD. Ms. Murillo earned her master's in social work at the University of Nevada, Reno.

Ms. Murillo works on developing capacity and sustainability of the reengagement programs within WCSD. Her work brings attention to the needs of youth who have left school and leads to programming that identifies early intervention strategies as well as supporting youth as they return to school. Ms. Murillo held a key role in the WCSD's first annual Student Voice Summit by facilitating a student panel addressing the importance of student voice within the reengagement process.

Tawnya Perry, Project Director, Los Angeles Unified School District, Pupil Services and Attendance, Diploma Project. With more than twenty years of experience working with at-risk youth in the Los Angeles Unified School District, Tawnya Perry has served as an administrator and overseen the development of programs for students who are at risk of dropping out of school and those who have been reengaged. Most recently, she served as project director for the U.S. Department of Education's fully funded High School Graduation Initiative Grant, The Diploma Project. She has taught at the University of California, Los Angeles, and the University of Southern California as an adjunct faculty member for ten years.

Perry holds a bachelor's degree in English from UCLA and a master's degree in social work from the University of Southern California. She has an administrative credential and a pupil personnel credential. She is also a licensed clinical social worker, who has previously had a private practice. She is married and has one daughter, who just graduated from Howard University. She believes that there is no work that can be as rewarding as making a positive impact on someone's life that ultimately enhances his or her future.

J. Weston Phippen, Staff Correspondent, *National Journal*, Washington D.C. J. Weston Phippen writes for *National Journal*, where he covers America's shifting demographics and how they are reshaping the country. He has written about everything from drug trafficking and cartel kidnappers to a family dedicated to keeping their daughter from becoming pregnant at sixteen—a problem the girl's mother, grandmother, and great-grandmother had all succumbed to. His work has appeared in *The Atlantic*, the *Los Angeles Times*, *Tampa Bay Times*, and *VICE*. He graduated from Arizona State University and grew up in Salt Lake City, beside the mountains.

Jennifer Poulos, Associate Director, Rennie Center for Education Research & Policy, Boston, Massachusetts. Jennifer has over a decade of experience in conducting and managing research and evaluation projects to examine critical federal and state education policy issues. Her career has spanned multiple sectors and has focused on effective policies and practices in students' transition from high school to college. Jennifer began her career at the U.S. Department of Education. She played key roles in several large-scale evaluations of federal reform initiatives focused on secondary school reform at Abt Associates and RTI International. At Jobs for the Future, she was a lead team member on a national postsecondary access and affordability initiative.

Jennifer has overseen the Rennie Center's research portfolio and is a lead researcher on many of the Center's research reports. In 2015, the Rennie Center partnered with the Boston Private Industry Council to develop a case study of the Youth Transitions Task Force—a cross-sector coalition supporting greater numbers of Boston youth in completing a high school diploma. Most recently, the Rennie Center profiled local early college models, including those serving at-risk and disconnected youth in setting college expectations. Jennifer holds a Master of Public Policy from Georgetown University, and a Bachelor of Arts from College of the Holy Cross.

Judy Rye, Director of Adult Education, Martha O'Bryan Center, Nashville, Tennessee. Judy Rye serves as the director of adult education and HiSET Chief Examiner at Martha O'Bryan Center in Nashville, Tennessee. She chairs the Alignment Nashville 16–24 Out of School, Out of Work team, which leads Nashville's reengagement effort. Judy began her career at the Martha O'Bryan Center in 2004 as the solo instructor, and now she is the manager of the Adult Education program that empowers and educates adults at all literacy levels. She is an advocate for innovation and collaboration and has presented at COABE's national conferences on best practices in teaching and program development.

Ms. Rye earned her Bachelor of Arts and teacher certification from the University of Tennessee, Knoxville. Her first career was in the theatre, and it is the skills she learned and practiced in this arena that have shaped her as a communicator, teacher, and leader. She and her partner, Dr. Paul Deakin, have a small, urban animal sanctuary and are committed to upholding and protecting the dignity and well-being of animals. Her daughters, Emma and Anna, are her "wonder women." Judy is currently at work on her PhD.

Robert Sainz, Assistant General Manager of Operations, City of Los Angeles Community Development Department, Los Angeles, California. During his time with the City of Los Angeles, Robert Sainz has been instrumental in reinventing the Workforce Development System, establishing the YouthSource System, and founding the LA Youth Opportunity Movement. He has impacted the lives of thousands of young people and adults, creating opportunities for them to return to school, enter employment, and start careers. Throughout his public service career, he has addressed many difficult social problems facing the community's low-income residents, including the challenges of juvenile delinquency, youth and adult unemployment, and poverty.

Robert is a Board Trustee and past president of the U.S. Conference of Mayors Workforce Development Council. He has received numerous awards and recognition for his work, including the Durfee Foundation's Stanton Fellowship. He received his Bachelor of Arts degree from UC Santa Cruz; Master of Public Affairs from Columbia University; and completed postgraduate work at the University of Southern California.

Alexander Thome, Director of Customer Success, Flocabulary, and former Director of Partnership Development and Reengagement, New York City Department of Education, New York. Alexander Thome was the director of Partnership Development and Reengagement for the New York City Department of Education's District 79 of Alternative Schools and Programs. He leads NYC's Referral Centers for High School Alternatives, which help thousands of students navigate their options and return to school each year.

Alexander studied at Santa Clara University as well as Columbia University's School of International and Public Affairs. He loves working to expand access to quality education and finding innovative solutions to public problems. He lives in Brooklyn, New York, with his greatest joys: his wife, Gabrielle, and his son, Jack.

The Honorable Martin J. Walsh, Mayor, City of Boston, Massachusetts. Martin J. Walsh took office as the city's fifty-fourth mayor on January 6,

2014. Mayor Walsh's vision is of a thriving, healthy, and innovative Boston—a city with equality and opportunity for all, where a revolutionary history inspires creative solutions to the world's hardest challenges. Since taking office, he has worked to create good jobs, great schools, safe streets, and affordable homes, while building a more responsive, representative, and transparent city government. He has won national recognition for expanding young people's opportunities and breaking new ground in community policing. And he has invited the people of Boston to help build a blueprint for the city's future in Imagine Boston 2030, the first citywide plan in half a century.

Before taking office, Mayor Walsh served in the Massachusetts House of Representatives from 1997 to 2013. Representing Boston's diverse 13th Suffolk District, he was a leader on job creation and worker protections; substance abuse, mental health, and homelessness; K–12 education; and civil rights. He played a key role defending Massachusetts' pioneering stand on marriage equality. Mayor Walsh also made his mark as a labor leader. Beginning in Laborers Local 223 in Boston, he rose to head the Building and Construction Trades Council of the Metropolitan District from 2011 to 2013. There he worked with business and community leaders to promote high-quality development and career opportunities for women and people of color.

Born and raised in the neighborhood of Dorchester by immigrant parents, Mayor Walsh is driven to make sure Boston is a city where anyone can overcome their challenges and fulfill their dreams. At age seven, Mayor Walsh survived a serious bout of Burkett's lymphoma thanks to the extraordinary care he received at Boston Children's Hospital and Dana Farber Cancer Institute. His recovery from alcoholism as a young adult led to his lifelong commitment to the prevention and treatment of addiction. And while working full time as a legislator, he returned to school to earn a degree in political science at Boston College.

Korinna R. M. Wolfe (Me-Wuk), Executive Director, Multiple Pathways to Graduation Department at Portland Public Schools, Portland, Oregon. Korinna is a social worker and educational administrator. As a social worker at Casey Family Programs from 1993 to 2003, she worked with children and families and collaborated for systems change at the local, state, and national level. Acknowledging the absence of culturally specific programming for Native American youth in foster care, Wolfe leveraged national nonprofit dollars to create a partnership that launched the NAYA Foster Care Program specific to the needs of American Indian and Alaska Native youth in foster care in Portland in 2002. She subsequently directed six programs for Native youth at the NAYA Family Center.

Since 2012, Wolfe has directed the Multiple Pathways to Graduation Department at Portland Public Schools, providing alternative education settings that empower, engage, and prepare students for college, work, and global membership and are tailored to the needs of specific student populations. Korinna enjoys the beautiful outdoors, and also reading, hiking, camping, and fishing with her family. Together, she and her husband most enjoy listening to their two middle school children play the tuba and saxophone and watching their two grown children enjoy adulthood and living happily in Portland, Oregon.